Financing Islamic Terrorism

Yves Dubitzky

CONTENTS

1 INTRODUCTION

"In February 1993 the apocalypse already seemed close in New York. Islamists staged an enormous explosion on a parking ceiling of the World Trade Center. Six humans were killed, hurt over 1,000. Only fortunate circumstances, static and weakness of the bomb prevented the first worst case of terror at that time."[1] Rolf Tophoven, the joint founder and deputy director of the Institute for Terrorism Research in Bonn seems to forget thereby two important components, which were missing for optimal success in 1993. On the one hand, this was the dilettante proceeding of the terrorists themselves, combined with former extremely generously arranged requirements of entry of the United States. On the other hand, this concerned a very secular aspect in the calculation of terror: the money, which was necessary for the preparation and execution of actions.

When 1995 the chief executive of the first terrorist attack on the World Trade Center, Ramzi Yousef, was arrested in Islamabad and hand over to the USA, he said during the over flight of the city of New York and watching the twin towers: "If I would have

---

[1] See Tophoven, Rolf (2002): Neue terroristische Strukturen: Osama bin Laden und die ‚Al-Qaida. In: Frank, Hans/Hirschmann, Kai (ed.): Die weltweite Gefahr: Terrorismus als internationale Herausforderung. Berlin , p.246.

1

had more money and time in order to build a larger bomb, the towers would not stand any longer."[2] Indeed, in the early 1990 years the financial structures of the terror network al-Qaeda must have been weakly trained in order to be able to effectively implement an attack on scale of the World Trade Center: „This self-sufficiency hurt the early cells of Al Qaeda, notably the first WTC bombing cell in 1993. In the early part of the 1990s, Al Qaeda did not have the necessary resources, or at least chose not to use them for its operational cells."[3] Nearly two years later, after his arrest in January 1995, Ramzi Yousef stressed again and again, when planning the attacks he would have had insufficient money: For example, he had to reject the plan to use poisonous gas and even the deployment of a truck would have been too expensive. A court observer therefore came to the conclusion that it concerns with the expressions rather statements. It might be possible that Yousef urged to make more money available for future attacks in order to guarantee the success of an attack.[4] His solicitation was to be given a greater voice...

Leading to the Topic

The attacks of September 11 2001 on the World Trade Center in New York and on the Pentagon in Washington meant a break in the history in each regard. Additionally, these simultaneously executed attacks expressed a new face of terrorism and helped it to get a new quality of its world-wide acting. But wherein lay the differences between the so-called new terrorism and the one before the mentioned, outstanding date in the middle of September 2001? Can also new quality criteria be anticipated

---

[2] Quoted after Mascolo, Georg/Holger Stark (2003): Operation Heiliger Dienstag. In: Der Spiegel 44, p.125.
[3] See Basile, Mark (2004): Going to the Source: Why Al Qaeda's Financial Network Is Likely to Withstand the Current War on Terrorist Financing. Studies in Conflict and Terrorism 27,
p.172. (Hereafter referred to as Basile 2004)
[4] See Emerson, Steven (2003): American Jihad: The Terrorist Living Among Us. New York, pp.51. (Hereafter referred to as Emerson 2003.)

regarding its financing from this "new" terrorism? Do risen incomes stand in correlation to effects?

The attacks or attempted attacks, as them the world public could observe in the past decade, are proof for it that the present form of the transnational acting terrorism is quite able to plan and to put into practice complex actions. This progress permits conclusions on structure and system of the newest generation of terrorist oriented groups, for which the Islamic al-Qaeda exemplary stands: Financial reserves and operational capital stocks, an improved infrastructure of terror and new ways of communication are indications of a clearly increased professionalization of the perpetrators.

The transnational terrorism represents particularly in its objective an advancement of the international terrorism.[5] While the international terrorism acted world-wide and occasionally entered into alliances with other local groups of terror; nevertheless, it pursued national goals. For the transnational terrorism, however, such geographical corset does not exist. The pretension of the terrorists became more global: To change the international situation is rather center of attention than focusing on a special region.

The development of the international terrorism has proven that with the expansion of the attacks to a global terrain the expenditures for planning and execution of such actions also rose accordingly. Particularly, the maintenance of training camps, the use of drugs and smuggling routes, the supply of retreat areas, and the warranty of smooth crossing borders with assistance of fraud passports and documents and the supply of the families of the assassins let boost the fixed costs of a terrorist organization. In the climate of the east west contrast, the

---

[5] See Schneckener, Ulrich (2002): Netzwerke des Terrors: Charakter und Strukturen des transnationalen Terrorismus. Studie der Stiftung Wissenschaft und Politik. Berlin, p.18. (Hereafter referred to as Schneckener 2002.)

terrorists willingly placed themselves under the protection of states and their secret services. First and foremost these included countries such as Libya, the Iraq, Iran or Syria in the Middle East. Precise differences could not always be identified in what sense it was the matter of a member of a terrorist organization or ordinary mercenaries, who were in the service of a government and its directives. The generation of money depended in most cases on where on the ideological range the individual terror organizations were. Nevertheless, the Palestine Liberation Organization (PLO) for example received benefits from non-governmental protagonists already at times of the Cold War.

Questions

The purpose of the work will be to indicate methods of the financing of the terrorism and a special attention will be directed to the presently most expressive form of terrorism, the radical Islamism. Referring to it the work deals with the following question: How does the Islamic terrorism finance itself? In this respect a number of further questions will arise:

1. What is generally understood by the term "terrorism"?

2. How about the financing of the terrorism in the past? Were there any differences to the today's methods of the financing? In this context: Does it make any sense to speak of a "new" terrorism? Were there tendencies to a privatization respectively a denationalization of the terrorism before the end of cold war?

3. What kind of connections exists between the political Islam, the Islamic financing sector and the Islamic relief organizations? Is the suspicion justified, which was openly expressed against some Islamic financial houses by the US administration? Which niches does the Islamic financing offer to the financing of terrorist organizations?

4. Which allegedly legal and illegal sources avail themselves terrorist oriented associations? What is the role of non-governmental actors of funding terrorism? Who are the protagonists and profiteers, i.e., who invests in political violence and who profits from it?

5. Given the increasing interdependence of terrorism and organized crime, is a separate combat of its financial resources still relevant and useful?

In my opinion, the objective of this paper is not to pursue the clandestine ways and dark channels of the terrorist financing to the smallest detail. This belongs to the jurisdiction of the police and secret service work and stands therefore outside of the range what can be achieved with this paper. In the literature in addition many different priorities are set, but just the straight facts are presented partially very contradictory: Is al-Qaeda actively involved in drug cultivation and trafficking narcotics as the team of writers Ray Takeyh and Nikolaus Gvosdev assumes?[6] Or does Osama bin Laden actually completely not participate?[7]

Basically the financing of the radical Islamism, at present the most acute form of the terrorism, differs from known groups in the past mainly in the fact that it stems both from apparently legal and illegal sources. About the private fortune of Osama bin Laden some is quite well-known. The data vary between 30 and 300 million US Dollar (USD).[8] Besides that, groups of terror rely on other apparently legal sources of income. This includes donations from private individuals. In addition, donations are collected by Islamic non-government organizations (in this

---

[6] See Takeyh, Ray/Nikolas Gvosdev (2002): Do Terrorist Networks Need a Home? The Washington Quarterly 25, Summer, pp. 97-108. (Hereafter referred to as Takeyh/Gvosdev 2002.)

[7] See Gunaratna, Rohan (2003): Inside Al Qaeda: Global Network of Terror, New York. (Hereafter referred to as Gunaratna 2003.)

[8] See Second Report of the Monitoring Group Established Pursuant to Security Council Resolution 1363 (2001) and Extended by Resolution 1390 (2002), S/2002/1050, 20.9.2002, p. 11.

context the development of Islamic financing is to be concerned) and passed on to local terrorist groups by means of to date unknown distribution code. Like the organized crime the terrorism has used similar methods to generate money: extortion, robbery, counterfeiting documents, the fast growing traffic of cigarettes, with which already more money is illegally acquired than with drug smuggling,[9] the traffic of diamonds or other jewels (particularly tanzanite) and the illicit trade in arms are included in the practices of terrorists. On the one hand, by transferring the funds the transnational terrorism profits from the globalization and the liberalization of the financial markets. On the other hand it can rely on some very old connections of ethnical clans among each other to transfer the funds beyond conventionally working banks through alternative transfer systems - summarized under the concept of the hawala transfer.

Structure of the Study

The funding practises of the Islamic terrorism essentially differ from active groups of terror in the past in three points. First, the portfolio of organizations such as al-Qaeda and Hezbollah is definitely higher than so far accepted. Secondly, such terrorist organizations avail themselves of clearly more complex transfer possibilities - partly through official, partly through unofficial ways. To third, the Islamic terrorism dissolved as far as possible from the state support and relies on the benefits of non-governmental players.

In the 1980s a process started where organizations like the PLO or the Hezbollah tried to free themselves continuously from the guardianship of the national patronage of rogue states as for example Iran or Libya. Examples of this early privatization of terrorism are the welfare organization Samed founded by PLO, which later developed into a commercial enterprise, and the

---

[9] See Neumann, Conny/Andreas Ulrich (2003): Rauchen für den Krieg. Der Spiegel 8, p. 82.

financial network consisting of donation incomes of the Diaspora and smuggling operations maintained by the Hezbollah. Both the PLO and the Hezbollah took pioneering role in concerning a privatization of the terrorism. In this respect, chapter three will be dedicated to the account of the financing of both organizations.

In the matrix of financing terrorism the Islamic terrorism prospected new sources. Illegally acquired funds represent only a part of the total revenue by criminal activities, which covered typically the basic needs of terrorist groups such as the Rote Armee Fraktion (Red Army Faction) in Germany or the Brigate Rosse (Red Brigades) in Italy. Al-Qaeda and the Lebanese Hezbollah almost perfected the privatization of terrorism in the recent time. They trust in an illegal as well as in an apparently legal generation of their funds.

Among the apparently legal sources, as described in chapter four, are in addition the investments of the al-Qaeda in Sudan and the private fortune of Osama bin Laden in particular donations from wealthy individuals as well as from the Diaspora. Donations from Muslims are religiously justified. To that extent, it is to be assumed that funds are either donated for the financing of a global jihad or for charitable purposes. In the period before the devastating attacks of September 11, 2001, sporadic Islamic banks and non-profit organizations were in the service of terrorist oriented groups like al-Qaeda. On the one hand, banks and relief organizations served the purpose of the donation acquisition, on the other hand with their assistance the funds were moved to the appropriate recipients. Chapter three will therefore deal with the structure of Islamic banks and relief organizations, and with the investments of al-Qaeda activated in the Sudan in the early 1990s.

Illegal sources (chapter five) are primarily revenue from criminal activities. Enclosed in it is among other things the smuggling of drugs, cigarettes and jewels. With this kind of generating, a separation of non-profit-oriented acting groups like terrorists and the organized crime is problematic. For the mutual benefit terrorism and organized crime adopt symbiotic relationships, although they pursue contrary objectives.

Groups of terror with a global radius of action are interested in the transfer of their funds in order to support affiliated cells. As chapter four will describe, Islamic banks and relief organizations serve to it. Besides, there are options to infiltrate funds into the official payment system of Western banks. Special attention is given on banks in so-called offshore centres which promise a maximum of anonymity for the investor. Alternative payment systems which are summarised in chapter six under the concept of the hawala transfer offer a further option for several terrorist groups to send money from point A to point B.

Chapters seven will serve for the final consideration and will give coevally a perspective, what can be done or has to be done against the financing of terrorism in the future.

State of Research

After the attacks of September 11, in the science the terrorism experienced a renaissance. The often edited topic, especially among the pioneers Walter Laqueur and Brian Jenkins, has been updated, referring mainly to the new manifestations of transnational terrorism. Up to the present time approx. 4,000 books, which have dealt with the topic "terrorism", have been published since 1979. In addition, innumerable articles come from magazines. A reason for the multiplicity of the publications is that the range of topics offers different starting points for research projects: Historical, cultural, religious, organizational or psychological moments within the problem can be attempts for different prospects.[10] Particularly, the papers deal quite in general with the questions about the structure of terrorist oriented organizations, the changing face of terrorism, what objectives terrorists pursue by their choice of attacks as a political weapon and about the role of the environment in which the terrorism prospers.

With all the variety, it cannot be ignored that some books are pure hard work, which unfortunately includes Udo Ulfkotte's book "Prophets of Terror"[11]. Textual, the book offers a wealth of facts and is also a helpful introduction to the topic. Yet one cannot help thinking that this is less a stringing together of his earlier articles in the German Frankfurter Allgemeine Zeitung. In his defense it must be said that Ulfkotte is one of the few German authors subjected the problem of financing terrorism.[12]

This might be justified in the fact that occasionally the stigma of unserious research adheres to the topic. As previously mentioned, sometimes it is difficult to distinguish between truth and "semi-truth" and the reader often tends to imply certain works or at least some parts of it as free invention. Most lightly, this problem can be documented in the person of Osama bin Laden. Either he is unmasked as a former agent of the US secret service,[13] what at the time of the Afghanistan war the service of Pakistan Inter-Service Intelligence (ISI) would have never admitted[14], or he is also described as a playboy[15] or alcoholic.[16]

---

[10] See Kiser, Steve (2005): Financing Terror: An Analysis and Simulation for Affecting Al-Qaeda's Financial Infrastructure. Santa Monica, pp. 13.

[11] See Ulfkotte, Udo (2001): Propheten des Terrors: Das geheime Netzwerk der Islamisten. München. (Hereafter referred to as Ulfkotte 2001.)

[12] To one of the few German titles that have explicitly dealt with the topic count: El-Samalouti, Peter (2004): Finanzierung des Terrorismus und Gegenstrategien. In: Hirschmann, Kai/Christian Leggemann (ed.): Der Kampf gegen den Terrorismus: Strategien und Handlungserfordernisse in Deutschland. Berlin, pp.201-234. (Hereafter referred to as El-Samalouti 2004.)

[13] See Labeviere, Richard (2000): Dollars for Terror: The U.S. and Islam. New York.

[14] Extent that as to speak as John K. Cooley states that "recently [...] Western investigations have revealed a second main channel for al-Qaeda funds, the [...] hawala system" is not without a certain arrogance to the reader.

About the person of the al-Qaeda leader can be written and be published anything popular – the authors will hardly face an action for slander.[17] Therefore, the suitability as scientific source is at least questioned and the difficulty of a literature basis to this topic is outlined: The offered facts are simply not verifiable since police or intelligence reports are not accessible. To that extent, in the present study will refer to articles from magazines (among others DER SPIEGEL, Newsweek) and the daily press (among others FAZ, New York Times, Washington Post), which form the basis of sources.

Some of the authors are only conditionally relevant as former employees of the secret service[18] or former administrative officers[19] and thus, if the work is designed as subjective memories without any presentation of evidence (e.g. Robert Bear). Beyond that numerous works of journalists exist [20] and of

---

Eventually, the US intelligence knew exactly how to take advantage of the by the FATF as Alternate Remittance System classified hawala transfers, just because a direct contact to fighting mujahedin was impossible during the Afghanistan conflict in the 1980s. See Cooley, John K. (2002): Hawala und Tansanit: Die flüchtigen Gelder der al-Qaida. Le Monde diplomatique No. 6905, 15.11.2002, pp. 16-17.

[15] See Bodansky, Yossef (1999): Bin Laden: The Man Who Declared War on America. Roseville.

[16] See Robinson, Adam (2002): Bin Laden: Behind the Mask of the Terrorist. New York.

[17] See Bergen, Peter L. (2003): Heiliger Krieg Inc.: Osama bin Ladens Terrornetz. Berlin, pp. 51. (Hereafter referred to as Bergen 2003.)

[18] See Scheuer, Michael: Through Our Enemies (2003): Osama bin Laden, Radical Islam, and the Future of America. Washington, D.C.. (Hereafter referred to as Scheuer 2003.); Scheuer, Michael (2005): Imperial Hubris, Dulles; Baer, Robert (2003): Die Saudi-Connection: Wie Amerika seine Seele verkaufte. Munich. (Hereafter referred to as Baer 2003.)

[19] See Clarke, Richard A. (2004): Against All Enemies: Der Insiderbericht über Amerikas Krieg gegen den Terror. Hamburg. (Hereafter referred to as Clarke 2004.)

[20] See Coll, Steve: Ghost Wars (2004): The Secret History of the CIA, Afghanistan, and bin Laden, from the Soviet Invasion to September 10, 2001. New York (Hereafter referred to as Coll 2004.); Adams, James (1990): Wer finanziert den Terror?: Die geheimen Geldgeber terroristischer Organisationen. Bergisch Gladbach (Hereafter referred to as Adams 1990.); Bergen 2003.

those, who have been temporarily active as journalists.[21] They supply the basis of facts and refer again to articles from magazines and daily papers or to the published reports of authorities.

At certain temporal intervals published reports of the authorities are considered as predominantly reliable sources. Among other things, the annual report of the US State Department "Patterns of Global Terrorism" belongs to such sources. Presently, similar reports do not exit in Germany. However, the in 2002 installed Financial Intelligence Unit (FIU) - resident at the German Federal Criminal Investigation Office in Wiesbaden and internationally informally summarised in the Egmont Group - publishes annual reports, which appear to be more realistic for being basic information. Same applies to the annual "Report on Money Laundering Typologies" of the Financial Action Task Force (on Money Laundering, FATF), which has provided the standard guidelines for the global fight against the financing of terrorism (Nine Special Recommendations on terrorist Financing) in conformity with the UN resolution 1373 (2001). Furthermore, the UN Monitoring Group created by UN resolution 1390 (2002) supervises the sanctions against al-Qaeda and related or associated organizations concerning their finances and hands over the report to the Sanctions over Committee installed by resolution 1267 (1999).

Scientific studies to the topic deliver the institutes. Here are to be called: the Washington Institute for Near East Policy (in particular the work of Matthew Levitt), the Middle East Institute and the Middle East Policy Council in the United States, the Israeli Institute for Counter Terrorism, the Rand Corporation with its head office in the Californian Santa Monica but also German institutes as for example the German Institute for International Policy and Security in Berlin as well as the German Orient Institute.

---

[21] See Emerson 2003.

As basis for the study serve also publications, which deal with the structure of Islamic banks and Islamic financing. Although such sources rarely consider the political background, a synthesis of financing and terrorism requires to be analyzed. As Wolfgang Hafner ascertained, in the United States the appraisals of foreign processes are only sporadically based on secret service inquiries - long ago these ratings were replaced by the knowledge of investment companies like J. P. Morgan.[22]

---

[22] See Hafner, Wolfgang (2002): Im Schatten der Derivate: Das schmutzige Geschäft der Finanzelite mit der Geldwäsche. Frankfurt/Main, p. 21. (Hereafter referred to as Hafner 2002.)

2 DEFINING TERRORISM

At present the term "terrorism" is made use so frequently that it could be assumed this concept would be unambiguously determined. Generally, terrorism is understood in the public reporting as a form of violence proceeded by non-governmental protagonists and the terms "terror" and "terrorism" are often synonymously used. However, clear statements about the structure of terrorist oriented organizations and above all about their political objectives are barely made. The actors of the international terrorism hardly work transparent. The same applies to the secret services which appeared since the initial years between 1960 and 1970 up to the end of the east west conflict as a crucial asset and help different organizations to its birth.[23] The international terrorism is subject to the respective political connotation; it is a political day-to-day interpretation, which varies every now an then and from government to government: By a political reversal, the former non-

---

[23] In particular, the concept of international terrorism is quite controversial. Peter Waldmann for example does not see any need for action to broaden the range of each terrorism (social revolutionary, ethnic-nationalist, religious, vigilante), as the "relevant criteria for distinguishing several forms of terrorism is the particular motivation and not the modalities for implementing an attack". See Waldmann, Peter (2003): Terrorismus. In: Nohlen, Dieter (ed.): Kleines Lexikon der Politik. Munich p. 525.

governmental ally might be the enemy of tomorrow. The decision whether freedom fighter or terrorist, is in the eye of the viewer.[24]

Even the suspicion of terrorism has become a tool of the policy. In the 1980s the British government accused the Irish Republican Army (Irish Republican Army) of terrorist action; however, the practices of the Palestine liberation organization (PLO) were classified as guerrilla warfare, which led to displeasure expressions on the part of Israel.[25] In 1998, e.g., units of the Kosovo Liberation Army (UČK) were officially designated by the US government as "terrorists" due to the fact that they targeted Serbian policemen and civilians. This changed with the following year: The USA decided jointly with the United Kingdom on an attack on Serbia. The former "terrorists" had thus become "freedom fighters".[26] These examples are to prove the fact that the term "terrorism" is with priority politically determined and must be politically defined.

The search for a generally accepted, all comprehensive definition has emerged as an insoluble assignment. The Dutch political scientist Alex P. Schmid took up this challenge and examined a total of 101 terrorism definitions according to 22 well-chosen criteria for its common characteristics.[27] About four years later, he repeated this process and had to state unsatisfied that the search has not finished yet.[28] Again, he found and selected 22 categories in order to filter the common characteristics of the definitions - with the same result: No definition used all 22 terms. 83.5 percent referred to force and compulsion, 65 percent came to the conclusion that the definition had to be a political

---

[24] See Kussbach, Erich (2003): Der Terrorismus und das internationale Strafrecht. In: Politische Studien 387, p. 63.
[25] See Adams 1990, p. 23.
[26] See Chomsky, Noam (2002): The Attack: Hintergründe und Folgen. Hamburg, pp. 64.
[27] See Schmid, Alex (1983): Political Terrorism. Amsterdam, pp. 119-158.
[28] See Schmid, Alex P. (1988): Political Terrorism: A New Guide to Actors, Authors, Concepts, Data Bases, Theories, and Literature. New Brunswick, p. 1.

one or at least implies the political aspect, and nevertheless, possibly half (51 per cent) of the selected definitions associated the term completely Aristotelian with fear and fright. Interesting, at this time only 6 percent mentioned the fact of a criminal offense.[29] What was approx. 50 years before still a main criterion for the classification of terrorism, degenerated to a marginal note in the end of the 1980s.[30]

Determination of Terrorism by the United Nations and the European Union

Crucial preliminary work for the fight against the financing of the international terrorism performed in 1999 from the UN general assembly accepted "International Convention for the Suppression of the Financing of Terrorism".[31] The convention was a result of a French initiative and was supported by the nations of the Group of Eight (G-8). It contains three obligations: 1. The signing states must include the passage of financing acts of terror as a criminal offense to their jurisdiction. 2. The states commit themselves to the international collaboration in this field. 3. The states agree to oblige financial institutions to order stop the financing of terrorist acts.[32]

The convention defined the terror financing as an offense, if a person wants „by any means, directly or indirectly, unlawfully and wilfully, provides or collects funds with the intention that they should be used or in the knowledge that they will be used in

---

[29] See ibid. pp. 5-6.
[30] In 1937 a special commission of the League of Nations submitted a "Geneva Convention for the Prevention and Combating Terrorism". This included the emphasis of terrorism as "criminal actions directed against a state and [its] objective to fear certain persons, a group of persons or the general public". However, no country except India ratified the agreement. See Heintze, Hans-Joachim (2000): Völkerrecht und Terrorismus In: Hirschmann, Kai/Peter Gerhard (ed.): Terrorismus als weltweites Phänomen. Berlin, pp. 218.
[31] See International Convention for the Suppression of the Financing of Terrorism. A/Res/53/108 (1999), 9.12.1999.
[32] For the current status of the convention see:
http://untreaty.un.org/english/bible/englishinternetbible/partI/chapterXVIII/treaty 11.asp.

full or in part, in order to carry out"[33] an act of terror, as it was specified in the convention before[34] and its conceptual determination is valid up to the present time.[35] The convention referred to the definition to nine international agreements regarding the fight against the terrorism.

With the internationalization of the terrorism, the search for the answer of the question, who is considered to be a terrorist, has attained an international-law meaning. As a result of faced crises, the UN Security Council considered the phenomenon of the international terrorism and its financing to be mastered. Since that time, the politics make every endeavour to find a generally valid definition, among other things with the purpose to border acts of terror as a criminal offense. Immediately after the attacks of September 11, one day later, the Security Council requested the member states in the resolution 1368 (2001) to proceed together against the international terrorism.[36] At the same time, this resolution implied also a refusal to politically and ideologically founded justification attempts of the international terrorism as part of the decolonization process. In 1972, a suggested definition of terrorism by the UN general assembly failed because of the resistance of the Arab and African states since an intended convention did not plan to differentiate between political actions in the context of national freeing wars and terrorist actions as such.[37] On 28 September 2001, the Security Council considered with the resolution 1373 (2001), to

---

[33] See International Convention for the Suppression of the Financing of Terrorism, A/Res/53/108 (1999), 9.12.1999, article 2, paragraph I.

[34] „Any act [...] intended to cause death on serious bodily injury to a civilian, or to any other person not taking an active part in the hostilities in a situation of armed conflict, when the purpose of such act by its nature or context, is to intimidate a population or to compel a Government or an international organization to do or to abstain from doing any act." See ibid. Article 2, Section I (b).

[35] See UN-Resolution 1566 (2004), S/Res/1566 (2004), 8.10.2004, Article 3.

[36] A complete list of all resolutions regarding this issue is available at: http://www.un.org/terrorism/sc/htm.

[37] See Warg, Gunter (2002): Terrorismusbekämpfung in der Europäischen Union. Speyer, pp. 17, 22.

understand the terrorism as a threat of the international peace and security.[38]

Less normative the European Union (EU) evaluated the expression "terrorist action" and named concrete acts, which accepted the criminal offense as terrorist, if a political motivation preceded the actions. In the "Common Point of View of the Council of 27 December 2001 about the Application of Special Measures to Fight the Terrorism", it was specified that there is an action of terror if the population of a country is intimidated or a government or an international organization is forced without justification "to doing or omitting". Furthermore Article 1 (3) iii) specified the criminal offenses, which have involved further definitions such as "terrorist association".[39] Indeed, an unequivocal definition of terrorism was evaded; however, a package of measures was determined which seemed to be more practically oriented and appeared to be more adapted to the domestic law. At the same time, however, the Ministers of Justice of the European Union presupposed that with each attack with obvious terrorist origin, a political motivation must exist. But what if attacks would be based on irrational motive like killing unbelievers, like religious mania?[40]

---

[38] „Reaffirming further that such acts, like any act of international terrorism, constitute a threat to international peace and security." See S/Res/1373 (2001), 28.9. 2001, p. 1.
[39] See Amtsblatt der Europäischen Gemeinschaften L 344, 27.12.2001, pp. 93.
[40] See Oltmanns, Jan: Definitions-Dilemma. Was ist Terrorismus? (http://tagesthemen.de/aktuell/meldungen/0,1185,OID3355742_TYP1_NAVSP M3~3572754_REF1,00.html). Visited on 10 September 2004.

Operationalization of the Concept of Terrorism

The present study will orient primarily by the definition which consists of the "threefold" components of the war handled by Carl v. Clausewitz: the military goal, the political objective and the used means. According to the understanding of the Prussian general, it corresponds to the nature of the thing that in a conflict, which he compared to a ring fight, the military goal can never dominate the political objective since the policy remains the origin.[41] Clausewitz could not anticipate that both coming, world-comprehensive wars, which were released under relevant (the First World War) and crucial (the Second World War) influence of Germany, should disprove his thesis of the dominance of the policy over the military to a large extent. As a kind of theoretical reinsurance from today's view, Clausewitz stated, however, the war as a "true chameleon", which changes "in each concrete case its nature somewhat".[42] That means, the character of war adapts to its environment and is in a constant process of development, conditioned by political changes, technological progress and cultural change, up to its present privatization.[43]

Christopher Daase tries to explain the today's phenomenon of the international terrorism with the mentioned "threefold" components of Clausewitz. Means, objective and goal would therefore possess a certain topicality, despite the loss of dominance of the policy over the military goals. Only three elements would have to be changed in addition: A political group uses military power against civilians (means)[44] in order to spread

---

[41] See Clausewitz, Carl von (2002): Vom Kriege. Hamburg, p. 218.
[42] See ibid. p. 23.
[43] See Münkler, Herfried (2003): Die Kriege des 21. Jahrhunderts. Gewerkschaftliche Monatshefte 4, p.193. Also see Cooper, Barry (2002): Unholy Terror: The Origin and Significance of Contemporary, Religion-based Terrorism. Studies in Defense and Foreign Policy 1, p. 8.
[44] If military constructions or soldiers are victims of an attack, their selection for being targeted did not result from military considerations.

fear, fright and panic (a goal) and to force the targeted state as the second participant to the change of its politics (purpose).[45]

For the consideration of financing terrorism in general it is important to separate the term of terrorism opposite to the organized crime as selectively as possible. Terrorists primarily do not work profit-oriented. They are not interested in the accumulation of the own capital. Their motivation is politically justified, even if they argue religiously. Their goal is the destabilization of a state and its mechanisms. According to a study of Loretta Napoleoni, the economic structures of the terrorism resemble those of a state, which redistributes the prosperity created by the nation in order the community functions.[46] In other words: Networks of terrorism derive their available finances from illegal (criminal activities) and apparently legal sources and distribute these, so that the global fight continues. The money is actually seen functionally by terrorist oriented groups as means for the objective.

---

[45] See Daase, Christopher (2002): Terrorismus und Krieg: Zukunftsszenarien politischer Gewalt nach dem 11. September 2001 In: Voigt, Rüdiger (ed.): Krieg – Instrument der Politik?: Bewaffnete Konflikte im Übergang vom 20. zum 21. Jahrhundert. Baden Baden, p. 369.
[46] See Napoleoni, Loretta (2004): Ökonomie des Terrors: Auf den Spuren der Dollars hinter dem Terrorismus. Munich, pp. 262. (Hereafter referred to as Napoleoni 2004.)

3 THE BEGINNING OF PRIVATIZATION OF TERRORISM

The religiously motivated terrorism experienced its true birth in 1979 and in the early 1980s years, when numerous terrorist organizations (HAMAS, Hezbollah) were founded, which felt legitimized by God. Besides, the year 1979 played thereby a crucial role. Directly several events stood godfather for the starting re-Islamization: In Teheran, the Shah regime was brought down; in immediate consequence Iran tried to export its revolutionary concept particularly to Palestine. In the Saudi Arabian city of Mecca radical Shiite extremists occupied the large mosque and the Kaaba using heavy infantry weapons. And in the December of the same year, the Red Army engaged in Afghanistan in order to assist the Soviet puppet government in Kabul.

The war in Afghanistan and its covert financing by the US American and the Pakistani intelligence had shown to the "warriors of God" (mujahedin) how a war could be financed by means of drug by creating smuggling routes through these also weapons and other goods reached the destination.[47] New, however, was the use of a so far unknown method of financing. Since the Islamic Conference in January 1981 was not able to agree to articulate a joint note to protest against the invasion of Soviet troops in Afghanistan, this function was adopted by religious networks from Muslim countries including the Muslim World League.[48] As a consequence, Islamic scholars drafted legal opinions *(fatwa)*, which should justify a war against the invaders resp. against the "unbelievers". In practice, this meant that in the following years thousands of Muslims flowed into the country in order to fight for the Islam. The Islamic organizations that were specifically established set up, in turn, offices in Pakistan to coordinate the flow of fighters, to take command of their recruitment and to enable their transfer across the border to Afghanistan as well as to deal with the influx of donations from the entire world, in particular from the Arabian hemisphere.

When the war was finished by the deduction of the Soviet troops in 1989, the USA stopped their weapon supplies; the networks of the Islamic organizations, however, remained intact. One of the co-ordinators of these offices was Osama bin Laden, who had led the "Afghan office" (Makhtab al-Kidmat) until 1989 together with his Mentor Abdullah Azzam in Peschawar.[49] Up to then bin Laden did not become obvious. Indeed, he experienced some front actions, but the status of a military or religious leader did apply to him. His profession were the finances - and so he was observed by the world up to the parallel attacks of Nairobi and Daressalam in 1998.[50]

---

[47] See Winchell, Sean P. (2003): Pakistan's ISI: The Invisible Government. International Journal of Intelligence and CounterIntelligence Vol. 16, No. 3, p. 379.
[48] See Kepel, Gilles (2004): Schwarzbuch des Dschihad: Aufstieg und Niedergang des Islamismus. Munich, Zurich, p. 175. (Hereafter referred to as Kepel 2004.)
[49] See United States of America vs. Usama bin Laden, et al. United States District Court. Southern District of New York, 6 Febuary 2001, pp. 187.
[50] In 1996 a dossier of the National Security Agency classified him as "one of the most significant financial sponsors of Islamic

The war in Afghanistan had developed its own dynamics and had helped the international terrorism to emancipate gradually from state benefits without completely renouncing it. Now, in the balance of payments of the terrorism a new item appeared: In addition to the subsidies the terrorist organizations received depending on their religious, ideological or political direction either from Teheran, Baghdad, Damascus, Tripoli, Washington or Moscow, the terrorists promoted their own kind of economy in order to demonstrate their independence. The PLO covered already in the 1980s a majority of their annual budget by an enterprise originally founded as a social institution called Samed and the Lebanese Hezbollah had installed its own financial network, which focussed primarily on the smuggling of goods of all kinds. In the following two chapters both cases will document the trend towards the privatization of the terrorism, which was already to be witnessed in the early 1980s.

PLO - Financing by Welfare Organizations

Far before the end of the Cold War, the state-financed terrorism was about to retire. A widespread common misconception was that terrorist groups were financed solely by government funds. This misconception primarily based on a book published in 1981 titled "The International Terror Network. The Secret War against the Western Democracies ",[51] which largely followed the logic of the Cold War. Claire Sterling represented the thesis in her book that the root of all evil is to be searched in Moscow resp. the Soviet secret service KGB. From today's view this work can be rated as propaganda. After its publishing it was rumoured that

---

extremist activities in the world today". See National Security Agency (1996): Usama Bin Ladin: Islamic Extremist Financier.

[51] "The KGB was directly involved, along with the secret services of the eastern European satellites of Russia. The role of the KGB is not object of speculation, but a documented fact." See Sterling, Claire (1983): Das internationale Terrornetz. Der geheime Krieg gegen die westlichen Demokratien. Bergisch Gladbach, p. 372. (Hereafter referred to as Sterling 1983.)

the CIA itself would be behind the book.[52] This case still documents, nevertheless, how much people give or wanted to give faith in the myth of state sponsored terrorism. Accordingly, the topic of the financing of terrorist oriented groups was also treated superficially. Asked about the financing of terrorism, we often received of suspect countries as a reply. First, this was the ideological enemy, as in the case of Sterling the USSR or Cuba, on the other, it concerned countries such as Syria, Libya or Iran.

In fact, terrorists need security in planning to perform their actions and to enforce the political objectives. Often thereby the role of a healthy budget is underestimated, i.e., long-term objectives require up to their implementation a long development stage and swallow correspondingly high development costs. Attacks of the scale of September 11 are not elaborated and planned within a period of a year.[53] The history of the destruction of the twin towers in New York did not begin only with the gradual seeping of the different groups into the United States, but - in the case of the group around the Egyptian Mohammed Atta - with their activation in Hamburg and the following training in camps in Afghanistan - years before.[54] As Kai Hirschmann stresses, terrorist motivated actions are not of spontaneous nature, but "premeditated" and "systematically planned".[55] The extent of an attack rarely meets a clear statement about its preparation. The hijacking of an airplane requires a similarly intensive research in the run-up (control of security measures at the airport, choice of weapons etc.) as, for example, its destruction. The fact that the preparations were successful and the terrorists were able to overcome the safety-relevant standards (for example, of an airport) points the success of the project.

---

[52] See Adams 1990, p. 14.
[53] See also Aust, Stefan/Cordt Schnibben (ed.): 11. September: Geschichte eines Terrorangriffs, Stuttgart, Munich.
[54] See Cziesche, Dominik (2002): Attas Armee. Der Spiegel 36, p. 112.
[55] See Hirschmann, Kai (2003): Terrorismus. Hamburg, p. 9. (Hereafter referred to as Hirschmann 2003.)

In the history of the internationally acting terrorism, state supporters have been proven more and more frequently as a bad contractual partner. With the guaranteed sums, which were paid rarely to the same amount and even more rarely in the same time intervals, the groups of terror could hardly plan in a longer term. States such as Libya behaved ostensibly as an official sponsor, but were in contrary to private donors extremely vulnerable to military interventions by the country which was affected by the terrorism (or by the international community). A government that supported terrorism financially and morally took a far larger risk than a "quiet" financier.[56] Moreover, the paid sums were disproportionate to the final product. In reverse, the terrorist groups were divided on the state support – too much did the investors dictate the wanted procedure to the terrorists.[57] Political independence was not to be achieved thereby, at least not as long as terrorists only behaved as some kind of marionettes for an ideologically or religiously related but still foreign power. From that point of view, it had to be the objective of each group of terror to reach the highest level of autarky in order not to abandon its political and military mobility. Besides it was not uncommon at all that state sponsors performed an intense foreign policy change or adapted to new political-climatic conditions that from formerly still promoted terrorists became criminals.

Despite all prejudices of the Palestinians to the Arabs and in reverse, it came to the national support of the PLO by countries such as Egypt, Saudi Arabia or Libya, which approached to the Palestinian organization by means of money for weapon

---

[56] On April 15, 1986 the United States bombed targets in Libya and justified the raid on the basis of the fact that the Libyan revolutionary leader al-Gaddhafi was said to be involved in the attack on the Berlin discotheque "La Belle" ten days before. The attack killed two people, 230 were injured. In 1998, however, the person of bin Laden was target of US air strikes in Afghanistan that were executed in the wake of the parallel attacks of East Africa. This also documents the trend toward privatisation of terrorism. See Bergen 2003, p. 59.

[57] See Grossbongardt, Annette (2004): Die Millionen der Hamas: Wie sich palästinensische Terrororganisationen weltweit ihr Blutgeld beschaffen. Spiegel Special 2, p. 102.

purchases.[58] Strengthened by a higher income from the sales of crude oil, the Gulf States were able to support the enemies of Israel financially. In November 1978 in Baghdad ten Arab government leaders met and submitted an annual support of approx. 3.5 billion USD for those countries that faced Israel hostilely. The sum should be split by the following distribution code: 800 millions went to Jordan, 250 to the PLO, the occupied areas of the Gaza Strip and West Bank should receive 150 millions and the rest and therefore the principal part were thus awarded to Syria. Signatories of this enormous sum were Saudi Arabia, the Iraq, the United Arab Emirates, Libya, Kuwait, Algeria and Qatar.[59] However, during the following years it remained a noble intention to support the Palestinian issue financially. Merely from Riyadh were to be expected sporadic payments and also these had to be sent a reminder occasionally.

More reliably, however, were donations from private individuals. Usually, the donations were made on the 29th of November, the day, which had been announced by the UN as the "day of the solidarity with the people of the Palestinians".[60] Referring to a report of the Beirut Middle East Reporter even in 1982 individuals from Saudi Arabia donated to the PLO. The then Secretary of Defence Prince Sultan Ben Abdel Aziz started with a donation of approximately 582,000 USD. He was followed by Prince Salman, emir and governor of Riyadh, and his deputy prince Sattam. The fact that behind the donations were not only moral aspects, but also economic interests, the case of Rafiq al Hariri, the later Prime Minister Lebanon has proven. He returned the favour with a gift of converted approximately 873,000 USD to the PLO since the Palestinians had not been the bar to the commercial interests of the then businessman al Hariri in Beirut. Among the donors were also numerous entrepreneurs - e.g. at

---

[58] See Hoffman, Bruce (2001): Trends in Outside Support for Insurgent Movements. Santa Monica, p. 36. (Hereafter referred as Hoffman 2001.)
[59] See Adams 1990, p. 112.
[60] See ibid. p. 114.

that time the in the Western hemisphere unknown Saleh Kamel, joint founder of the Dallah al-Baraka.[61]

Altogether since 1973 the PLO received estimated 100 million USD a year from donating countries, so it they could rely on a yearly revenue of approximately a quarter billion USD. Though, the fixed costs accounted to approximately 500 million USD.[62] Due to this fact that voluntary donations could hardly be calculated, the PLO had to look around for alternate options in order to prospect new pecuniary resources.[63]

The PLO was just as little homogeneous at its prime zenith as the today's al-Qaeda is. Back in the early 1980s, the organization of the PLO can be compared structurally and organizationally with an international company, whose subsidiary companies acted relatively independently.[64] The PLO functioned thereby only as a controlling body for each single terrorist oriented sub-groups, which had partially own sponsors, as in the case of "black September". Despite the admission of individual Fedaijin groups into the Palestinian Liberation Army and despite the creation of a united supreme command, the single groups of terror remained independent. They planned own actions and searched for state sponsors mostly in the Gulf region, which made them on the one hand dependent on the investors, on the other hand, however, uncontrollable by the PLO supreme

---

[61] See Palestinians Aid. Middle East Reporter, 11 May 1982.

[62] See Sterling 1983, p. 364.

[63] 1991 Arafat had bitterly experienced how it is to opt for the wrong side. Prior to the Iraq war, the Palestinian leader had voted for Saddam Hussein what caused very few receptions mainly on the Arabian Peninsula. As a result, the flow of money from Arab countries dried up and was redirected to strengthened Hamas. From now on, the value of the so-called persistence funds (*amwal al-sumud*) that the PLO had invested in the Palestinian territories fell from initial 350 million USD to 120 million in 1990. In 1993, the value had reached 40 million USD. Many institutions had to be closed which had a sustainable negative impact on the backing of the PLO in society. See Kepel 2004, pp. 384, 510.

[64] See Adams 1990, pp. 99.

command.[65] As an extreme case the so-called Abu Nidal Group is to be named. Abu Nidal, whose original name was Sabri al Banna, had fell out with his former combat companion Yassir Arafat on the issue of the radical nature of the practice of the struggle against Israel and emphatically rejected all peace negotiations with the Hebrew country. Subsequently in the middle of the 1970s fights between Arafats al Fatah and Nidals "Black June" inflamed in which Arafat himself was targeted of some attacks. The Nidal Group had lost its former terrorist character and commuted particularly to the Iraq and Syria in the 1980s, by offering its services (among other things weapon supplies to the Iraq) to the respective governments. So Nidal created thereby a dubious name as a group of mercenaries. This generally raised the question what differs terrorists from mercenaries, if they receive their financial support by a state.[66]

Especially in the beginning, in the early 1970s, it seemed important to Arafat to prove political credibility particularly to the state of Israel by internal cohesion of the organization. In addition, the organization was to be built on a solid financial foundation. For this reason in 1970 the Samed, the labour organization for Palestinian martyrs, were established which was directly subordinated to the Palestine National Fund. One purpose of the organization was to be the bundling of the manpower in the refugee camps and the construction of a first still rudimentary economic infrastructure of the Palestinians. At the beginning limited to Beirut, the organization rapidly expanded to other refugee camps.[67]

---

[65] See Büttner, Friedemann (1998): Die PLO und die palästinensischen Fedaijin-Organisationen bis 1976 In: Der große Ploetz: Datenenzyklopädie der Weltgeschichte, Freiburg im Breisgau, p. 1569.

[66] As a terrorist mercenary group the Abu Nidal group has an amazing financial cushion which is composed of profits from real estate and business investments. At the end of the 1980s, the organization could look back at a very successful decade: In 1988, the assets of the Nidal group were estimated to be worth of 400 million USD. See Hoffman, Bruce (1999): Terrorismus – der unerklärte Krieg: Neue Gefahren politischer Gewalt. Frankfurt/Main, p. 251.

[67] See Kometer, Michael W. (2004): The New Terrorism: The Nature of the War on Terrorism. Alabama, p. 35.

Objective of the Samed was to bundle unused workers in the refugee camps and to establish the PLO as economically independently, self-sufficient. Initially conceived as a welfare organization, the Samed became a business enterprise, which had realized profits into millions of US dollars, which had exported goods and which had opened new branches in the Arab area and in Africa. Fundamental idea was the supply of the camps with textiles (e.g. blankets) and of the PLO with uniforms. There were production plants in every Palestinian camp, in which the workers enjoyed benefits such as work premiums or life insurances. At the beginning the Samed was still dependent on gifts from foreign countries, e.g. knitting machines from East Germany or Romanian wood, but within shortest time, it established and achieved own profits. However, the industrial sector gained a turnover of approximately 18 million USD in the year of 1982.[68]

Beside the industrial sector the Samed was divided into three further departments: Media (i.e. production of documentary films and movies, in other words propaganda department), agriculture as well as trade, responsible for import and export of raw materials and goods.[69] Since Israel insulated its own market by high tariffs on Palestinian manufactured goods from the occupied areas and in addition these goods could be imported only with special permission into Israel, the Samed appeared as a broker and mediated import and export contracts for Palestinian goods, which were mainly delivered to the USSR or to Arab states.[70] In particular, the agricultural sector became so enormous

---

[68] See Adams 1990, pp. 166.

[69] See Khella, Kharam (1982): Der israelisch-arabische Konflikt: Über Krieg und Frieden im Nahen Osten, Hamburg, pp. 176.

[70] In science the concept of „internal colonialism"was introduced for it, which describes the connection of capitalism to pre-capitalist production methods: "The consequence of this link is that the capitalist system is supplied of labour which are reproduced in a pre-capitalist system, and therefore, represent an extremely cheap production factor for the capitalist system since the labour do not have any indirect taxes or costs for social security have to be provided." See Sunderbrink, Ute (1993): Die PLO in der Krise? Genese, Strukturmerkmale und Politikmuster der Palästinensischen

that the Palestinian charity maintained huge farms (mainly poultry farms) in Africa, which came to an annual profit of about 16 million USD.[71]

This progress continued until 1982. Up to then the Samed employed approx. 200 permanent employees in Syria and approx. 1800 in Africa. Nevertheless, the production core was focused on Lebanon. There were approx. 5000 permanent and 6000 part-time workers, who were spread over 35 factories.[72] The (second) invasion of Israel in 1982 was a temporary shock for the organization. The Samed, which were smashed in Lebanon as far as possible, had to change to countries such as Algeria, Syria or Tunisia. But the organization remained relatively unimpressed by the events in Lebanon. In 1986 the gross revenues reached again an amount of 39 millions compared to 45 million USD in the year 1982 and in 1989 the Samed achieved the point of approx. 70 million USD.[73] Altogether, the amount of direct investments of the PLO in farms, arms and clothes factories, real estates and newspapers amounted according to a report of the British National Intelligence Service 1994 over ten billion USD.[74] Additionally, until 1993 the Samed relied on annual guaranteed 50 million USD, which resulted from the "Palestine Liberation Fund Tax" - a kind of revolutionary tax of five percent of the income of all Palestinians world-wide; possibly comparably with the techniques of the Basque Euskadi ta Askatasuna (ETA).[75]

The Samed and its establishment in the Palestinian camps show that long before the end of the Cold War were ambitions to break away from a national patronage. Its own economic power

---

Befreiungsorganisation und deren Herausforderung durch den politischen Islam in der Intifada. Münster, Hamburg, p. 65.

[71] See Napoleoni 2004, p. 124.

[72] See ibid. p.124.

[73] See ibid. p.125.

[74] See Ehrenfeld, Rachel: Where Does the Money Go? A Study of the Palestinian Authority, October 2002
(http://www.intelligence.org.il/eng/bu/financing/articles/where/where.htm).
Visited on 16 June 2005.

[75] See ibid.

as well as a solid financial foundation contributed to an identity formation, likewise as the starting dissociation from outside control by foreign funds did. Therefore the PLO was in a position to define its political objectives independently. Payments from Arab states were often attached to concrete conditions, besides they were most unreliable and mostly never steady. The situation was different in the relations to private donors, almost entirely businessmen, who conditioned their benefits quite to economic interests, as the case of Rafiq al Hariri has proven. Saleh Kamel who was classified in 1982 in the report of the Middle East Reporter as "not identified", despite the fact that he founded the Dallah al Baraka Group in the Saudi Jeddah in the same year, holds shares of important banks in the Palestinian autonomy areas. Today he is accused of supporting the Hamas financially by means of the al Aqsa Islamic Bank.[76]

Hezbollah - From State Sponsored Terrorism to Private Financing

The first-time candidacy for the Lebanese parliament in 1992 and the withdrawal of the Israeli troops from Lebanon in the year 2000, the leadership of the Hezbollah got into serious argumentation trouble. Originally designed to counter the Israeli occupying military forces the organization was divided whether it should continue to support radical elements or further strengthen the social commitment in the Middle East.[77] A central issue represented the support from abroad. For large parts of the Diaspora it was more important to financially support the ideology of an armed resistance rather than the political legitimization efforts forwarded since 1992.[78]

---

[76] See Rosenbach, Marcel/Michael Wulzinger (2003): Arabische Liga. Der Spiegel 6, p. 71.
[77] See Katzman, Kenneth: Terrorism. Near Eastern Groups and State Sponsors, 13 Febuary 2002 (CRS Report for Congress), p. 4.
[78] See Meehan, Howard Vincent (2004): Terrorism, Diasporas, and Permissive Threat Environments. A Study of Hizballah's Fundraising Operations in

Despite the fact that the Hezbollah covers the majority of its financial needs by funds from Iran - the organization of the party of God ("Hizb Allah") receives estimated 100 to 200 million USD annually from Iran - the leadership is still anxious to achieve financial and hence political independence from Teheran.[79]

One of the most important sources of income of the terrorism is smuggling. For this purpose terrorist organizations co-operate with local syndicates or are involved in these businesses and become part of a smuggler economy, in which shocking profits are gained. A special kind of a financial centre is the Paraguayan Ciudad del Este - originally established by the former president Stroessner in order to benefit from that about ten million tourists, who pilgrimage to the Iguaçu falls every year.[80] The Hezbollah has excellent contacts to Latin America. In this respect, Ali Khalil Mehri, a from Lebanon immigrated Paraguayan businessman, sold software pirate copies, which had been illegally imported from Asia to Paraguay, amounting to millions of US dollars, and sent the money to the Hezbollah. Altogether, by this means, about 330 to 500 million USD are said to have left the Tri-Border Area (TBA) heading to the Middle

---

Paraguay and Ecuador. Naval Postgraduate School. Monterey, p. 11. (Hereafter referred to as Meehan 2004.)

[79] Regarding payments from Iran to Hezbollah (and Hamas) contradictionary numbers are available. The majority of the sources mention the sums between 100 and 200 million USD as stated above. Even in the mid1990s there was talk of a decline in payments that were said to be only at 60 million German Mark at that time. The Iran was increasingly becoming pushed into the background and private Arab sponsors had taken precedence. This could also help to explain why al-Qaeda could easily cooperate with the Hezbollah and the Arab Diasporas in South America for short or long term. See Ulfkotte, Udo: Bildet Teheran in geheimen Lagern 5000 ausländische Terroristen aus? Frankfurter Allgemeine Zeitung, 8 August 1996, p. 6; Geld für Terroristen aus den Golfstaaten. Frankfurter Allgemeine Zeitung, 16 August 1996, p. 5; Förster, Andreas: BND sucht verstärkt nach Finanzquellen der Terroristen. Berliner Zeitung, 26 October 2001, p. 7.

[80] See Seri, Guillermina S.(2003): On Borders and Zoning: The Vilification of the "Triple Frontier". Prepared for Delivery at the 2003 Meeting of the Latin American Studies Association. Dallas, p. 2. (Hereafter referred to as Seri 2003.)

East to various organizations that have built a South American "branch".[81]

Transfers to the Middle East predominantly come from Lebanese, who live in Africa or South America resp. maintain business there. For providing a good example, which documents the facts, is the crash of an airplane of the Union Transport Africaines, flight 141 in Benin on December 25, 2003. Among the dead were also three Hezbollah members, who carried approx. two million USD of donation funds from Africa. The Israeli intelligence rates Senegal and the Ivory Coast among those countries, in which the Hezbollah fundraises most of its money.[82]

Beside Africa, South America, particularly Paraguay counts to the main centres in the financing circulation of the Hezbollah: The transfers from the Diaspora are meant as donation funds for relatives, whose members are fallen in the fight against Israel, even if this were always denied by the local authorities in South America.[83]

The Hezbollah uses relief organizations to mask its own fundraisings, even if it depends less on annual benefits from Iran due to own illegal businesses rather than the Hamas does. Indeed, the example of the al Aqsa International Foundation illustrates that a clear separation of the cover organizations, which are responsible for collecting of donation funds, is nearly impossible: According to statements of an in Germany arrested and to the USA extradited Yemeni Sheikh Moayad, formerly managing director of the al Aqsa International in Yemen, individual branches of the alleged relief organization (in the

---

[81] See Napoleoni 2004, pp. 272.

[82] See Levitt, Matthew (2005): Hezbollah: Financing Terror through Criminal Enterprises. Hearing of the Committee on Homeland Security and Governmental Affairs United States, Washington, D.C., p. 5. (Hereafter referred to as Levitt 2005.)

[83] See „Washington vermutet Terrorzellen in Südamerika" Frankfurter Allgemeine Zeitung, 19 October 2001, p. 8.

meantime prohibited) foster al-Qaeda as well as Hamas and Hezbollah.[84] Organizations, which support the Hezbollah financially, do not have to belong necessarily to the financial terrorist network. Partially, also an ideological affinity of the Islamic institutions is an essential object for terrorist organizations. The Islamic Resistance Support Association, the al Shahid Fund, the Educational Development Association and the Goodwill Charitable Organization in the USA, the al Shahid Organization in Canada, the Karballah Foundation for Liberation in South Africa, the Lebanese Islamic Association and the Welfare Committee, the al Shahid Social Relief Institution in Germany and the British Jam'iyat al Abrar rank among those organizations.[85] Beside the aspect of fundraising donations, the Islamic relief organizations have yet another meaning within the considerations of the terrorists: Frequently employments in the organizations serve the terrorist as cover. Thus one of the bombers of the September 11 attack testified that he told his family, he would in future work for the International Islamic Relief Organization.

The Hezbollah is involved in numerous criminal businesses around the globe. Among their activities rank both the trade with smuggled goods (including drugs and above all diamonds from East Africa) as well as all kinds of fraud (e.g. credit card fraud, falsification of documents). Particularly in this field in the past,

---

[84] On January 10, 2003 the Yemeni Sheikh Mohammed Ali Hassan al-Mujjad and his secretary Mohammed Moschen Jahia Sajjid were arrested in Frankfurt/Main (Germany) and then delivered to the United States. The Imam of Sanaa's main mosque and an important member of an opposition party in Yemen was accused of having close contacts to bin Laden's al-Qaeda and its supply of money, weapons and voluntary fighters since 1997. Apparently the US investigators were more interested of al-Mujjad's relationship to bin Laden at the time of his seizure. His well-known ties to Hamas were no determining factor for his arrest despite the fact that he apparently granted nearly 3.5 million USD to Hamas through the al-Aqsa Foundation. Another 20 million were supplied to bin Laden. See Holm, Carsten (2003): Hilfe für den großen Bruder. Der Spiegel 3, p. 34; Mascolo, Georg (2003): Verdächtig gezuckt. Der Spiegel 4, p. 37; Wassermann, Andreas (2003): Quelle CI1. Der Spiegel 27, p. 48.
[85] See Levitt 2005, p. 7.

ad-hoc-alliances with other well-known groups of terror have been have been occurred, also including al-Qaeda.[86] To the Hezbollah applies, which applies to any other groups of terror: there is hardly to find a criminal method, which is not used by the terrorists. It is partially difficult to distinct terrorism from the organized crime. In June 2002, the case of a Hezbollah cell became known in the city of Charlotte in North Carolina. The investigations proved that the cell was not only restricted in its actions to the American continent. The network of cigarette smuggling and money laundering even reached to Europe, where falsified documents were provided which was needed for the entry of additional members from Lebanon.[87] Although false passports may mean a criminal act of lesser intensity, but the actual possession of a US passport is just for residents of the Middle East a special temptation as only a travel document such as this enables all transfers required by terrorists.[88]

With the search for funds the Hezbollah also enters into alliances with the organized crime. A genuine conurbation of various radical-Islamic groups from the Near East is the Paraguayan city of Ciudad del Este in the Tri-Border Area (Paraguay-Brazil-Argentina, TBA) in South America. Up to the attacks of September 11, 2001, basically no border controls existed along

---

[86] See Winer, Jonathan M. (2002): Globalization, Terrorist Finance, and Global Conflict In: Pieth, Mark (ed.): Financing Terrorism, Dordrecht, Boston. London, p. 26. (Hereafter referred to as Winer 2002.) About cooperations between al Qaeda and Hezbollah there are only few reports. However, there should have been meetings in 1994, at which had al-Qaida and Hezbollah agreed to a joint use of training camps in Lebanon and Sudan according to al-Fadl's testimony in the trial against the attackers of East Africa. See United States of America vs. Usama bin Laden, et al. United States District Court, Southern District of New York, 6 Febuary 2001, p. 288.

[87] See Levitt 2005, p. 4.

[88] According to Steven Emerson, it is possible that Osama bin Laden even endeavoured to US American visa during his stay in Sudan in 1993. It is a fact, however, that his borther in law, the Jordanian Mohammed Jamal Khalifa quite successfully managed to enter the USA in 1994. Only after US authorities discovered that this man was on trial at home, he was arrested and extradited to Jordan. Besides him, a Saudi of Yemeni roots tried to entry as well. His identity is kept secret by the US State Department. This individual should be constituted as Osama bin Laden. See Emerson 2003, pp. 156.

this area. Cooperations between terrorist oriented groups and parts of the organized crime remained unconsidered for a long time, so that smuggling, money laundering or arms traffic had been accepted and become traditional.[89] Money juggler from the Middle East got employed by the local white-collar crime to launder its illegally gained profits from drug businesses. That is why groups especially from Colombia and Peru meet in Ciudad del Este. These groups take advantage of CC5 accounts offered by the Brazilian national bank to foreign individuals, originally mentioned to speed up transfers of Paraguayan funds onto Brazilian accounts.[90]

For the first time the Hezbollah attract the world's attention on the South American continent by two attacks: On March 17, 1992 a bomb assassination on the Israeli embassy occurred in Buenos Aires, which meant at this time as the largest anti-Semitic attack outside of Israel since the end of World War Two. Two years later, on July 18, 1994, another assassination attempt on a Jewish community centre, the Argentine Israeli Mutual Association (Asociacion Mutual Israeli Argentina, AMIA), likewise in Buenos Aires, with 86 humans were killed, 200 more were injured.[91] Both attacks were quickly linked to the Hezbollah through the person of Imad Mughniyah.[92] The authorities, however, did not realize before May 2003 who exactly was behind the attacks: Assad Ahmad Barakat, at the time of the attacks resident of the Paraguayan Ciudad del Este. He was supposed to be both financier and logistician who supported the preparations with imported material (C4 plastic explosives) and volunteers (two or three Lebanese suicide bombers). In the years

---

[89] In October 2001, the Brazilian President Cardoso disagreed with a US American proposal to establish an anti-terror unit, as saying that "in this region a focus of terrorism does not exist". See „Washington vermutet Terrorzellen in Südamerika" Frankfurter Allgemeine Zeitung, 19 October 2001, p. 8.

[90] See Bartolome, Mariano Cesar (2002): La Triple Frontera: Principal Foco de Inseguridad en el Cono Sur Americano. Military Review July-August 2002, p. 67. (Hereafter referred to as Bartolome 2002.)

[91] See Steinitz, Mark S. (2003): Middle East Terrorist Activity in Latin America. Policy Papers on the Americas Vol. XIV, Study 7, July, p. 6.

[92] See Gunaratna 2003, p. 220.

1990 and 1991, Barakat is said to have made several journeys to Iran in order to meet there with high-ranking officials of the Islamic republic. In the same period, he also travelled to Lebanon, probably for recruiting volunteers.[93]

A tie of the South American group of the Hezbollah to the al-Qaeda cannot undoubtedly be verified. However, since approx. 1999, South American secret services observe a rapprochement between local groups and al-Qaeda.[94] One reason could be that the Iranian government is less involved in this region. This vacuum has been filled by al-Qaeda, as local authorities assume. A concerted police action on December 22, 1999 in all three larger cities of the TBA, Ciudad del Este, Foz Do Iguaçu and Puerto Iguazu revealed that al-Qaeda and Hezbollah had jointly planned attacks against Jewish institutions in Argentina and Canada.[95] The contact is said to have been established by Imad Mughniayh, who owned the dubious predicate of the world's most dangerous terrorist until September 11, 2001, and according to some experts had model function for bin Laden's terrorist raids.[96]

Beside the Hezbollah, the Egyptian Gamma'a al Islamiyya, the Palestinian Hamas and also al-Qaeda (since 1999) rank among the radical-Islamic groups resident in the TBA. Primary operating

---

[93] See US-Departement of the Treasury (2004): Treasury Designates Islamic Extremist, Two Companies Supporting Hizballah in Tri-Border Area, 11 June 2004.
[94] More detailed about the link between Hezbollah and al-Qaeda resp. Mughniayh and bin Laden: See Junger, Sebastian (2002): Terrorism's New Geography. Vanity Fair No. 508, December, pp. 200-202.
[95] See Hudson, Rex (2003): Terrorist and Organized Crime in the Tri-Border Area (TBA) of South America: A Report Prepared by the Federal Research Division, Library of Congress under an Interagency Agreement with the United States Government, Washington, D.C.,
p. 16. (Hereafter referred to as Hudson 2003.)
[96] More about the person of Imad Mughniayh and his life: See Goldberg, Jeffrey (2002): In the Party of God: Hezbollah Sets Up Operations in South America and the United States. The New Yorker, 28 October 2002 (http://www.newyorker.com/fact/content/articles/021028fa_fact2). Vistited on 30 August 2005.

field of these groups is the financial support of the respective organizations in the Middle East. Largely, the funds derive thereby mainly from drug business, arms trafficking, falsification of documents, product piracy, the active money laundering, extortion or the simple collecting of donation funds in the Arab communities of this region.

By the Hezbollah is well-known that in addition to state subsidies from Iran, the drug traffic in the Syrian controlled Beka'a valley, the donation acquisition and the diamond trade in Africa, the TBA is of one the main pillars of its annual income.[97] Besides, the Hezbollah is said to have formed strategic alliance with al-Qaeda in the TBA. So one of the men, who had already tried to blow up the world trade centre in New York in February 1993, was Adnan Marwan al Qadi (also known as Marwan al Safadi), member of the Hezbollah.[98] Even more concrete became the cooperation of the Hezbollah with the organized crime in the TBA. With a volume of estimated twelve billion USD of "laundered" funds per year, the Paraguayan Ciudad del Este, the former Puerto Presidente Stroessner, and the neighbouring Brazilian Foz do Iguaçu are third biggest centre for the world-wide money laundering among Miami and Hong Kong.[99]

It is generally supposed that in the TBA and in similar foreign trade zones of Latin America (among other things the Colombian Maicao, the Chilean Iquique or the Venezuelan Isla Margarita) per year about 200 to 300 million USD are passed on to radical groups in the Middle East, which were gained by drug business, smuggling of arms or product falsification.[100]

---

[97] See „Angriffe auch auf Lager der Hizbullah?" Frankfurter Allgemeine Zeitung, 29 November 2001, p. 4.

[98] In November 1996, with regards to the attempted attack on the US embassy in Paraguay al-Qadi was arrested in Asuncion by local authorities, extradited to the United States and there sentenced to 18 months in prison. Yet he was sent to the Canadian justice and sentenced to nine years in prison. After several failed attempts, he managed to escape from prison, and via detours he finally arrived to Ciudad del Este. See Hudson 2003, p. 77.

[99] See ibid, p. 3.

[100] See ibid, p. 4.

In the mid-1970s, during the civil war in Lebanon, the Hezbollah and other Islamic organizations had begun, to open up the region of the TBA due to its relatively large Arab Diaspora. The TBA served as place of refuge for the planning of attacks, for cooperation with other radical groups as well as for the financial support of the basic organization in the Middle East. Up to the present time nothing has changed. On the contrary, as Bruce Hoffman of the RAND Corporation stresses expressly, the influence of the Diasporas on the radical-Islamic organizations in the Middle East will even rise due to their financial meaning in close future.[101] Already before the attacks of September 11, 2001, Reuven Paz of the Israeli Institute for Counter-Terrorism referred in a remarkable article to the fact that the radical-Islamic groups in the Middle East would increasingly rely on the financial support by the Diaspora. He calls this the "Islamic atmosphere", a kind of "greenhouse" for groups of terror.[102]

Generally the number of the Arab Muslims, who reside in the TBA, varies between 20.000 and 30.000, whereby the majority of them is spread over the two cities Ciudad del Este (approximately 240,000 inhabitants) and Foz do Iguaçu (approximately 190,000 inhabitants).[103] About 90 percent of them are of Lebanese origin and predominantly originate from the Beka'a valley.[104] However, in consideration of lax entry

---

[101] "Diasporas may become more important to insurgencies in the future because, unlike states, they are more reliable in funding and do not seek to exert control over a movement. In addition, ethnic insurgencies, which are growing in number relative to ideological ones, have an already-established bond with immigrant communities that they can exploit." See Hoffman 2001, p. XV.

[102] See Paz, Reuven (2000): Targeting Terrorist Financing in the Middle East: Paper Presented at the International Conference on Countering Terrorism through Enhanced International Cooperation Courmayeur, Mont Blanc, Italy, 24 September 2000. (http://www.ict.org.il/articles/articledet.cfm?articleid=137). Visited on 22 April 2005.

[103] See Mendel, William W. (2002): Paraguay's Ciudad del Este and New Centers of Gravity Military Review March-April, p. 53. (Hereafter referred to as Mendel 2002.)

[104] See Curtis, Glenn E. et al. (2003): Nations Hospitable to Organized Crime and Terrorism: A Report Prepared by the Federal Research Divison, Library of

controls by the countries Paraguay, Argentina and Brazil, it is to be assumed that the number of those, who are illegally in the TBA, might be by far higher than officially accepted. For the Lebanese government the importance of the community in South America is that mighty that it has closed its embassy in Asuncion in 1999 and opened a consulate in Ciudad del Este.[105]

Since the Arab community in South America got into the focus of attention of the Hezbollah - at the same time with the start of the political commitment in Lebanon and the succeed in entering parliament, the leaders of the Shiite and now also politically legitimized as "party of God" found almost ideal conditions in the TBA.[106] Back in the early 1970s, the government in Asuncion tried to profit more efficiently from the tourist attraction of the Iguaçu falls and promoted for this reason the region to a free trade area in which Brazilians and Argentines were permitted to buy cheap goods. Hoping to strengthen the own economy by open borders and by lax controlled entry requirements, both terrorists and organized crime were likewise invited to attend to their illegal businesses more easily by gotten these new liberties.

Ciudad del Este or generally the TBA in South America, belong to those areas on earth, which are alternatively described either as "lost geographies",[107] as "area gris",[108] as "failing states",[109] as "permissive threat environment",[110] as "lawless area"[111] or as

---

Congress under the Interagency Agreement with the United States Government, Washington, p. 175.
[105] See ibid. p. 176.
[106] In 1994, the spiritual leader of Hezbollah, Sheikh Fadhallah visited the Arab community in the TBA fort he first time. From then on, the commitment of Hezbollah on the South American continent began. As it is known by other radical-Islamic groups, the Hezbollah uses especially local mosques for the fundraising of donations and the distribution of its ideological basic structure. See Meehan 2004, p. 35.
[107] See Mendel 2002, pp. 51-57.
[108] See Bartolome 2002, pp. 61-74.
[109] See Rotberg, Robert I.(2002): The New Nature of Nation-State Failure. Washington Quarterly 25 (Summer 2002) 3, pp. 85-96. (Hereafter referred to as Rotberg 2002.)
[110] See Meehan 2004.

"brown zones".[112] Paraguay rates according to Transparency International among to the lowest position (together with Azerbaijan on position 140) of the annually published list, i.e., the South American country has one of the most corrupt government world-wide.[113] So, e.g., in September 2001 the Paraguayan consul of Miami, Carlo Weiss was arrested who had sold about 300 visas, passports and similar papers from June 1999 to 2001 and had thus made possible 16 presumed terrorists from Egypt, Syria and Lebanon to enter Paraguay.[114] The average price of a falsified passport amounts to about 5,000 USD - in this manner estimated 570 persons are to enter the country at the river Parana per year.[115]

Although only approx. 150 km away from the capital, Ciudad del Este developed in the course of the years to a "failed area", i.e., the region along the borders to Brazil and Argentina has evaded completely the control by the central power. Thereby, Paraguay joins the world-wide list of those countries, to which the status "failing state" is awarded and which act as an operational base, place of refuge and logistics centre for the internationally active terrorism.

If countries like Somalia break down, sub governmental protagonists replace the original state. They seize control of certain regions or of the entire territory of the former state and

---

[111] See Taylor, Paul D. (ed.) (2004): Latin American Security Challenges: A Collaborative Inquiry from North and South. Newport.
[112] See O'Donnell, Guillermo (1993): On the State: Democratization and Some Conceptual Problems, (A Latin American View with Glances at Some Post-Communist Countries.), Working Paper No. 192 (University of Notre Dame. The Helen Kellogg Institute for International Studies, April 1993). (Hereafter referred to as O'Donnell 1993.)
[113] See Transparency International Corruption Perception Index 2004 (http://www.transparency.org).
[114] See Rohter, Larry (2001): Terrorists Are Sought in Latin Smuggler's Haven. New York Times, 27 September 2001, p. A3.
[115] See Bartolome, Cesar Mariano (2002): La Triple Frontera desde la perspectiva argentina: principal foco terrorista den el Cono Sur americano, 7 August 2002 (http://www.geocities.com/mcbartolome/redes2002.htm.). Visited on 12 August 2005.

create their own economic infrastructure for the assertion of a shadow economy, which is primarily based on the trade in weapons, humans, jewels and natural drugs. In this respect, these created shadow economies of the individual failed states or regions appear to a considerable point compatible with networks of terror.

But not in all cases the political authority collapse completely as for example in Somalia - it is rather the exception.[116] On the other hand, the number of states with sinking political influence on the own territory is by far higher. To these so-called failing states belong countries such as Colombia, in which the central government is at least still able to maintain a certain control of single areas.[117]

The presence or intensity of violence actually makes no statement about whether a state is failed or not. Rather it is the persistent character of the violence, which is directed against the existing government and lay claims to the separation of power or an entire autonomy in order to justify its existence. In contrast to conventional states with a strong central power, failed states have no considerable control of their own borders. Usually, the national influence is limited to the seat of the government resp. the capital or maximally to some other zones. The majority of the country avoids a national influencing control. In fact, the regional control of the state of its country is one of the indicators for a failed state: Who really controls the country - particularly with larger distances to the political epicentre - and supervises the observance and realization of the legal stipulations?

---

[116] At present Robert I. Rotberg of the Kennedy School's Programm on Intrastate Conflict counts seven countries to which the criteria of a failed state apply: Angola, Burundi, Liberia, Democratic Republic of Congo, Sierra Leone and Sudan. See Rotberg 2002, pp. 90.
[117] See Foxell, Jr., Joseph W (2003): The U.S. War on Terrorism: Prospects for Success? American Foreign Policy Interests 25, pp. 90. (Hereafter referred to as Foxell 2003.)

Another indicator is the control of the organized crime particularly in the densely populated zones, the large cities. The more national power shrinks, the more gangs and criminal syndicates control the trade on the street. Under these conditions the trade with drugs and weapons thrives, since it is limited in its activities by no police measures. Usually police officers are involved and profit also from the structure of an "economy in the shade".[118]

For terrorist groups it is of high importance that a state has not broken down completely yet. Individual regions represent the ideal fertile soil for terrorism, in which the political central power does not possess influence, therefore present neither with police nor with military means. But not always does an accurate characteristic result that suggests a failing or failed state. As in the case of Pakistan,[119] e.g., up to a point not all the criteria apply to Paraguay which is mentioned by Rotberg as characteristic of the political failure. For this reason, it seems appropriate to expand the mentioned definition of Rotberg of failed states to certain areas. Failed areas are therefore zones, over which the state has no appreciable control, without the state has failed as a whole. The supply of the citizens with political goods functions continues, and the direct political influence is not only limited to the capital. Nevertheless, there are areas, in which the state possesses neither a functional nor a territorial presence. According to Guillermo O'Donnell, director of the Helen Kellogg Institute for International Studies, these are so-called brown areas. His colour palette extends from blue over green to brown. "Blue" represents a high functional and territorial presence of the state in all geographical areas of its country.

---

[118] See Rotberg 2002, pp. 85.
[119] "These types of conflict however are not characteristic of the Pakistan situation. No serious and organized popular challenge to state authority exists, nor do people question the basis for the organization of the Pakistani state and its ideology. The attempted car bombings against President General Musharraf by Islamic extremist groups at the end of 2003 also do not suggest any impending failure of the Pakistani state." See Mohan, Raja C. (2004): What If Pakistan Fails? India Isn't Worried...Yet. Washington Quarterly, 28, p. 119.

Green would be all those areas, which the state has penetrated territorially, but not functionally. On the other side "brown" areas would lack in presence of both dimensions. Therefore e.g. Norway would be characterized as blue, the USA would consist of blue and green zones (though with some brown points in the urban areas and parts of the south) and countries such as Brazil, Peru, Paraguay or Argentina were completely dominated by brown, but with variable intensity of that colour. All together, O'Donnell remarks, that the total number of the "brown" zones is rising.[120]

Referring to Michael Hardt and Antonio Negri the moral intervention is usually followed a military one, which is presented to the world's public as an internationally sanctioned police action.[121] Interestingly terrorism and drug trade are the most frequent mentioned causes for world-wide interventions - and the TBA, particularly the Paraguayan Ciudad del Este unites both factors. But where is an interference of the USA, which stressed in March 2002 in person of President Bush's emissary Grossman facing Argentine president Eduardo Duhalde that the global fight against the terrorism in Afghanistan and the Middle East could be easily expanded to regions like Colombia and the TBA.[122] After the USA used up both their military and its moral resources in the war against the Iraq and particularly in the desired nation building, it might take some time until the administration in Washington will deal actively with the situation in South America - knowing about the danger of an imperial overstretching as described by Paul Kennedy.[123] Four years after the attacks in New York and Washington the fight against the terrorism and its sources seems to stagnate.

---

[120] See O'Donnell 1993, p. 11.
[121] See Hardt, Michael/Antonio Negri (2003): Empire. Die neue Weltordnung. Frankfurt/M., New York, pp. 53.
[122] See Seri 2003, p. 9.
[123] See Kennedy, Paul (1994): Aufstieg und Fall der großen Mächte: Ökonomischer Wandel und militärischer Konflikt von 1500 bis 2000. Frankfurt/Main.

For a long time the presence of terrorist groups from the Near East in Latin America has been ignored. Addressed to the obvious problem, the local authorities relativized and insinuated that there are no connections between the organized crime and terrorism in this region.[124] Correspondingly the attacks of 1992 and 1994 were treated unworried. Due to permeable frontiers, which actually exist only in the maps, the terrorists shifted their places of residence depending upon necessity and arranged among other things the investigative authorities of the three bordering countries to blame mutually the blame for investigation mishaps.

With the occurrence of September 11, 2001 and its well-known consequences, the US American pressure to the governments in the TBA was increased. The financial support of terrorist oriented organizations was installed as a criminal offense in the respective legislations, financial instruments like the mentioned CC-5 accounts were invalidated, borders controlled more strictly, various anti-terror units came into being as well as numerous persons were arrested and partly extradited to the USA.[125] The efforts of the legal stipulation might be only marginal in the future, if the national authority is limited to the capital in a country such as Paraguay.

If the United States want to remain internationally reliable in their proclaimed "war on terrorism", then they will be forced to get involved more strongly and show presence, where the problems are so obvious and the local authorities either not able or not willing to fight these actively. Moreover, the USA will not get by to grant to regions like the TBA highest priority in their fight against the transnational acting terrorism if radical-Islamic groups like

---

[124] See Madani, Blanca (2002): Hezbollah's Global Finance Network: The Triple Frontier. Middle East Intelligence Bulletin Vol. 4, No. 1, January 2002 (http://www.meib.org/articles/0201_l2.htm). Visited on 31 August 2005.
[125] See United States Department of State (2004): Patterns of Global Terrorism, April 2004, pp. 78.

the Hezbollah should furthermore profit from the absence of national power, because the potential violence and the required financial power, might be barely smaller than in the case of al-Qaeda.

4 FINANCING TERRORISM FROM LEGAL SOURCES

In Egypt of the early 20th century, interest-free bank accounts were offered by then founded postal savings banks already. In 1963 economical expert Ahmed al Najjar accomplished an experiment, in which he tried to integrate the savings deposits of lower classes into the economic circulation, which were distrustful to the established banks.[126] For this purpose, in the rural city of Mit-Ghamr in the Nile delta a savings bank was instituted, whose business methods completely depended on the economic principles of Islam. In other words, the poorest ones obtained bank credits free of interest (*qard hasan*), while the wealthier ones, who looked for possibilities of investment and shared the chance of profit and the risk of loss with the financial

---

[126] Ahmed al-Najjar had studied social economy in Germany and returned back home to Egypt in the early 1960s. Once there, he tried to adapt the German savings bank model to Egypt and to establish it on a long-term basis. For this purpose, he contacted German investors who supported the project from now on and for the progress of the bank, a loan of 780,000 German Mark was contributed. See Soliman, Samer (2004): Rise and Decline of the Islamic banking model in Egypt. In: Henry, Clement M./Rodney Wilson (ed.): The Politics of Islamic Finance. Edinburgh, p. 267. (Hereafter referred to as Soliman 2004)

backer (profit-and-loss-sharing).[127] With this concept of profit-and-loss-sharing (*mudaraba*) the financial backer (bank) and the investor (entrepreneur) participate of the profit to a degree resp. to a proportion, which was arranged before. In the case of loss the banks bore a part of the risk according to its in brought capital as well.[128] In addition, the savings bank introduced a special *zakat* fund, which made two and a half percent of the capital available for the needy ones. In 1968 the project were stopped after a political intervention of the state; in 1971 at the instigation of Sadat the Nasser Social Bank was founded and so that this was the national succeeding organization of the experiment in the Nile delta. Although not expressly named as an Islamic bank, this bank adopted tasks, which corresponded approximately to the savings bank project of al Najjar as well: The allocation of interest-free credits, the *zakat* collecting (stipulated by the Qur'an as alms tax) and its summary in funds, and the allocation of production-loans on easy terms. This reestablishment of a national bank, named after the old president, included also a clear political statement: Sadat wanted to break the monopoly of the Islamists, who were involved preferentially in the social sector.

It seems to be important to note that between the Egyptian savings bank model (and its succeeding institution, the Nasser Social Bank) and other Islamic banks certain differences existed and exist. Mit-Ghamr and the Nasser Social Bank, which was subordinated to the Ministry of Social Affairs and had expressly no religious authority, were closely linked to the Egyptian socialism under President Nasser. In particular, the project of al Najjar would have to be regarded as social under the banner of Islam. However, Al Najjar had no reason not to cooperate with conventional banks and not to make business with it. On the other side, Islamic banks intend to disqualify conventional banks

---

[127] See Kepel 2004, p.191.
[128] See Wippel, Steffen (1995): „Islam" und „Islamische Wirtschaft": Vertreter des religiösen und politischen Islam und der islamischen Wirtschafts- und Wohlfahrtseinrichtungen in Ägypten, Berlin, p. 3.

to its Muslim clientele since these banks work on basis of interests (*riba*), which is according to the interpretation of the Qur'an ethically and religiously not justifiable.[129]

The Evolution of Islamic Financing

The upswing of Islamic financing is closely connected to the Arab peninsula and originated at a time of the antagonism between the United States and the Soviet Union during the Cold War. In this respect, the Islamic financing possessed special connections to the political Islam since its establishment.

Within the Arab and Islamic world Saudi Arabia ascended to an important ally of the USA owing to its rising oil income, while Egypt took up a key role on the side of the Soviets. In both countries the Islam was integrated into the political rhetoric and was introduced in geopolitical considerations. At this time Nasser in Egypt pursued the Muslim Brotherhood, which is considered as genesis of all modern Islamic movements whereas Saudi Arabia offered political asylum to its most important leaders.

With the support of the United States Saudi Arabia tried to declass the Egyptian Pan Arabism (closely connected to the name of Nasser) by founding the first modern pan-Islamic movement, the Muslim World League in 1962.[130] Pilgrimages to the Islamic sanctuaries in Mecca and Medina were additionally used to strengthen contacts with important leaders of the Islamic world. In order to form a counter project to Nassers solidarity with the Arab countries and countries of the so-called third world, the then Saudi Arabian king Faisal announced the concept of the Islamic solidarity. Primarily financial assistances for non-

---

[129] See Soliman 2004, p. 269.
[130] See Warde, Ibrahim (2004): Global Politics, Islamic Finance and Islamist Politics Before and After 11 September 2001 In: Henry, Clement M./Rodney Wilson (ed.): The Politics of Islamic Finance, Edinburgh, p. 38. (Hereafter referred to as Warde 2004.)

Arab Islamic countries in Asia and Africa were a significant component of this new doctrine.[131]

A number of incidents promoted Faisal's position and with that the concept of the Islamic solidarity. These included the complete Arab defeat in the Six-Day War in June 1967, in its consequence the Pan Arabism was seriously questioned, and the October War in 1973 (in Arab named as Ramadan War and in the Hebrew Israel as Yom Kippur War), which was in contrast completely marked by a religious symbolism.[132] Already in the mid-1970s, the pan-Islamic solidarity was considered as a powerful movement – headed by the financial patronage of Saudi Arabia. Increasingly, countries that had before only rare connections to the Arab world, such as Pakistan, Indonesia or Turkey, integrated the thought of the pan-Islamic solidarity into their considerations of foreign policies. Among other things, financial assistance by the oil exporting Saudi Arabia ranked with that. But these monetary backings were closely linked to certain demands on behalf of the Arabs, because the countries were committed to import the Arabian variety of Islam, the puritanical Wahhabism. The introduction of religious tribunals as well as the use of the Islamic jurisdiction, the Sharia, became in this way distinctively honoured.[133]

Starting from 1975 the increasing influence of Saudi Arabia on the Islamic financial world became completely apparent with the establishment of the Islamic Development Bank. On the summit of the Organization of the Islamic Conference in the Pakistani

---

[131] See ibid.

[132] The 6th October, when the raid named „Operation Saladin" was conducted, is also the tenth day of the fasting month of Ramadan on which the Prophet Mohammed started his holy war against Mecca and its military leader Saladin in 630. But the 6th October is the most prominent holiday in Israel as well (Day of Atonement). Sadat considered this as good conditions to win the upcoming war against the Jewish neighbours. Eight years later, his assassins should pay their respect to the very same day in reverse. See Krautkrämer, Elmar (2003): Krieg ohne Ende? Israel und die Palästinenser – Geschichte eines Konflikts, Darmstadt, pp. 68.

[133] See Napoleoni 2004, p. 198.

city of Lahore in 1974, a resolution for the establishment of an Islamic Development Bank maintained by all signatory governments were adopted. Primary objective of the bank was the splitting of the oil revenues in the Gulf States among the members of the Islamic Conference by a certain distribution code.[134] 44 states signed as initial members. The largest shareholders were Saudi Arabia (with a share of 25 percent), Libya (16 per cent), the United Arab Emirates (14 per cent) as well as Kuwait (13 per cent). One year later in the Saudi city of Jeddah the financial institution was founded. The two Saudi main initiators, Prince Mohammed al Faisal al Saud and the businessman Sheikh Saleh Kamel, the later founders of the supra-national holdings Dar al Mal al Islami (literal: "Islamic financial house") and Dallah al Baraka ("fortune") urged to the establishment of an Islamic bank.[135] From now on the Islamic financing represented which had already begun after the Six Day War: The secular pan-Arab movement of Nasser was at the end and Saudi Arabia became executive, which - also owing to the risen oil price - increasingly wished to exercise its claims in the Arab region.

In the following years, particularly at the beginning of the 1980s, numerous banks arose. These included the Saudi al Rajhi Banking & Investment Corporation, the already mentioned Dallah al Baraka and Dar al Mal al Islami, the Finance House in Kuwait, International Islamic Bank in Qatar, the Dubai Islamic Bank as well as the bank Muamalat in Malaysia. In 1979 as the first country, Zia ul-Haq put the Pakistani financing under the regulation of the sharia. Iran and the Sudan followed the example of Pakistan in 1983.[136] An exception formed Malaysia, where likewise Islamic banking laws were used, however, existed besides the conventional banking system. In 1983 the Malayan parliament under the in 1981 elected Prime Minister Mahathir

---

[134] See El-Samalouti 2004, p. 205.

[135] See Warde, Ibrahim (2000): Islamic Finance in the Global Economy, Edinburgh, p. 75. (Hereafter referred to as Warde 2000.)

[136] See Siddiqi, Moin A. (2002): Banking on Shari'ah Principles. In: The Middle East, July/August, p. 34.

Mohammed (1981-2003) approved an Islamic Banking Act, according to which the first Islamic bank of the country, Islam Malaysia Berhad bank was founded. Ten years later, the Malayan government permitted conventional banks to offer Islamic financial instruments for service.[137] Principal motivator of this rather progressive interpretation of Islam ("modernized Islam") in Malaysia though was the vice Prime Minister Anwar Ibrahim, who interpreted the religious conditions in the meaning of a national development model. Malaysia was to become a center both for the Islamic religious community and for the international economy.[138] Generally, the Islamic banking system faced the problem to take up international conditions of the financial markets without insulting thereby the Islamic law, which contained a prohibition of interest (*riba*).

The Prohibition of Interest: *riba*

The Islam does not offer a canonical law, which would correspond roughly to the Christian canon. The Qur'an refers expressly to a prohibition of interest revenue. Sura 2, verse 275 says: "Those who charge usury are in the same position as those controlled by Devil's influence. This is because they claim that usury is the same as commerce. However, GOD permits commerce and prohibits usury."[139] It remains unclear whether the term *riba* is to be translated generally with interest or with an exorbitant rate of interest.[140] Interest or exorbitant rates of

---

[137] See Warde 2000, pp. 126.

[138] See Ufen, Andreas (2004): Islam und Politik in Südostasien: Neuere Entwicklungen in Malaysia und Indonesien In: Aus Politik und Zeitgeschichte B21-22, p. 17.

[139] According to Gilles Kepel, the prohibition of interest has also a philosophical dimension, because if someone ever wants to protect himself of bad surprises with the help of previously agreed interest, is not bending to the will of Allah. For the same reason the is no insurance coverage in Islam. See Kepel 2004, p. 190.

[140] A similar problem shows the etymology of the English word "usury". The related Latin word usura (plural usurae) stands for "interest" or "income" in general. This reminds of similar bans in the early days of Christianity. Literally the Sermon on the Mount in Luke 6,34-37 says: "If you loan things to people, always expecting to get something back, should you get some special praise

interest are only concepts of *riba*, that means literally translated "accumulating". Textually, the concept refers to each kind of unlawfully made profit, which results from a numerical disparity of the equivalents - or any party of an agreement benefits finally much more highly from a trade or a deal than the other one does. Already in early periods of Islam financial transactions were carried out on the basis of mutual partnerships between the backers and the debtors, who purchased their goods on loan. Both profits and losses were shared, i.e., businesses of this type were embedded into partnership connections.

These ideas of an "ethical" financial law kept safe to a great extent in the respective enterprises of the present. The modern Islamic banking system focuses on partnership models of jointly borne profits and losses.[141] Yet, Islamic banks could never conceal the dilemma, how cope with a world, in which the return of investments has utmost priority. For this reason, Islamic financing was very early endeavoured to search for alternative techniques, which located beyond interest behaviour. Volker Nienhaus, professor for economics, counts to it purchasing and leasing transactions: "So a financial transaction becomes a real business in which no interest, but an extra charge for a payment extension or payment by instalments is demanded. Economically, there are no considerable differences between interest and an extra charge, but legally spoken there is one."[142] Additionally,

---

for that? No! Even sinners lend to other sinners so that they can get back the same amount! I'm telling you to love your enemies and do good to them. Lend to people without expecting to get anything back. If you do these things, you will have a great reward. You will be children of the Most High (God). Yes, because God is good even to the people that are full of sin and not thankful. Give love and mercy the same as your Father gives love and mercy."

[141] The so far seemingly unreachable savings have been remained unnoticed of the Western financial houses for a long time. In the meantime, many of the big banks provide special services for Muslim customers. Financial heavyweights such as Barclays, Deutsche Bank, Commerzbank, Credit Suisse and HSBC have set separate niches – so-called Islamic windows - in order to recruit Muslim clientele. See Siddiqi, Moin A. (2004): Islamic Investment. In: The Middle East May, p. 38.

[142] See Nienhaus, Volker (2002): Islam und Staatlichkeit. Zur Vereinbarkeit von Religion, Demokratie und Marktwirtschaft. In: Internationale Politik 3,

those people were expected to be reached, who refused cash transactions for religious reasons.[143] An opportunity was to be given to them to feed their saved money in the financial system. This also included that banks would fulfil the purpose of the alms tax *zakat*, and would left a part of profits to philanthropic institutions in accordance with the Qur'an.[144]

Similar to other fiscal systems, numerous types of duties and taxes are also well-known to an Islamic state. This includes the mandatory tax for the poor (*zakat*, *saddaqah*), which in turn

---

p. 17.

[143] To this end, in the early 1980s the Islamic Housing Co-operatives were founded in Canada. Many Muslims of the Canadian immigrant community were denied to purchase a house because local banks only offered interest-based loans. The cooperative model, which was developed by the Director of the Islamic Center of Canada, presented a way possible way out, and is now also exported to countries like Pakistan, New Zealand, the UK or Saudi Arabia. This model differs fundamentally from the usual way of a loan. To join the cooperative, members buy shares of equity pools. Once a member has accumulated a certain amount of shares, the cooperative buys the house and the family moves in. Then the family pays a proportional rent to the cooperative: For example, has the owner of the house contributed 20 percent to the price of the house and the cooperative the remaining 80 percent, so the purchaser pays the 80 percent to the cooperative in the form of the rent. From the date of the moving in, the purchaser has further to invest in shares of the cooperative. The more is invested, the lower the rent is – until the payment finally expires. Similar to other models in the Islamic finance, this is also based on partnership with the motto: Money does not generate money. See Sanford, Jeff (2004): Muslim Profit. In: Canadian Business, 27 September 2004, p. 39. – Recent examples of Turkish holdings prove that there are also black sheep among those firms offering Islamic-compliant services. More than 200,000 Muslims living in Germany invested large amounts of their savings in Turkish companies (including Yimpas, Jetpa, Kombassan), and they never saw their money again. See Fröhlingsdorf, Michael (2004): Neuer Markt auf Türkisch. In: Der Spiegel 5, p.36.

[144] Ibrahim Warde of he Harvard University perceives the Islamic concept which sets great store on alms duty and redistribution of wealth, as a counterbalance to the current dismantling of the welfare state in the Western hemisphere. In addition, alternative funding models have proven to be highly innovative. The conventional wisdom, after which the Islam is said to be paralyzed and less adaptable to new ideas, is simply wrong. See Warde, Ibrahim (2001): Eine unwahrscheinliche Erfolgsgeschichte. In: Le Monde Diplomatique, 14 September 2001, p. 5.

represents one of the "Five Pillars of Religion".[145] Back in the early days of Islam, the devoutness did not only concern the spiritual relationship to God, but the Qur'an was expected to regulate the solidarity among the faithful. Soon the mandatory tax for the poor (*zakat*) and the voluntary alms tax (*saddaqah*) emerged.[146] Normally, the *zakat* is about 2.5 percent of the net income.[147] A large part of the annual *zakat* is donated especially to charities, mosques or schools during the Ramadan (*zakat al fitr*).[148]

To monitor the observance of Islamic laws, a so-called Sharia Supervisory Board is superordinated to each bigger enterprise. This supervisory board examines among other things whether the transacted trade corresponds with the laws of the Sharia.[149] A business is considered as dubious if it is related to pork, tobacco, alcohol or pornography.[150] As reference for the behaviour of

---

[145] The „Five Pillars of Religion": 1. The belief of one God and of Mohammed, his prophet. 2. The duty of praying after taking a ritual bath five times a day. 3. The sharecropping of an alms tax due to the income. 4. The fasting in the ninth month (Ramadan). 5. The pilgrimage to Mecca.

[146] See Heine, Peter (ed.): Lexikon des Islam Vol. 1, pp.25.

[147] In addition to *zakat* and *saddaqah* for Muslims, there is a so-called compensation tax (*jizya*) for non-Muslims. This serves as a compensation for non-Muslims who are not subjected to the compulsory military service and who are further not applied to the jihad. Nevertheless, it is up to non-Muslims to participate in military service or to pay the *zakat*. See Khatab, Sayed (2002): Citizenship of Non-Muslims in the Islamic State of *Hakimiyya* Espoused by Sayyid Qutb. In: Islam and Christian-Muslim Relations Vol. 13, 2, pp.181.

[148] See Abdelkarim, Riad Z. (2004): After Year of Uncertainty: American Muslim Charitable Donations Rebound. In: Washington Report on Middle East Affair Vol. 23, January/February, pp.62-64.

[149] This also applies to non-Islamic banks offering services to Muslims. In this manner, the al-Sukoor European Equity Fund of the Commerzbank is endorsed by the Sharia Advisory Board of the Dallah al-Baraka Group. This collaboration may not be without any problems, at least, the Dallah al-Baraka Group belongs to those companies that are subject of a prepared US civil action against various Saudi banks, charities and individuals at US District Court for the District of Columbia. Among other things, the in 1982 in Jeddah established company is accused of an investment in bin Laden's Sudanese branch in Khartoum.

[150] See Rosly, Saiful Azhar (2005): Critical Issues on Islamic Banking and Financial Markets. Islamic Economics, Banking and Finance, Investments,

Islamic banks the "Handbook of Islamic Banking" was published in 1977, including prohibitions of derivative financial instruments such as futures or options. Islamic banks were urged to refrain from any short-term stock and commodity business as well.[151] If such participation is discovered by the Sharia Board yet, the profits completely convey to charitable foundations.

The Role of Islamic Banks in the Financing of Terrorism

By emphasising the *zakat*, Islamic banks had also influence on the financing of Islamic relief organizations, which regarded it as its common task to spread the Saudi variety of Islam all over world and to occasionally finance Islamic movements. From that it becomes evident why banks and relief organizations after the attacks of September 11, 2001 got into a general suspicion of financing terrorism: Islamic banks retain automatically the above mentioned alms tax with each money transfer and with each transacted business. The appropriate amounts are then passed on to charitable foundations. The *zakat* transfers do not appear in public balance sheets of the bank and cannot be traced by investigating authorities.[152] As soon as the transfer for instance to a charitable institution has finished, all documents will be destroyed, i.e., the payments can be passed on to Islamic groupings indirectly through affiliated charity organizations such as the International Islamic Relief Organizations (IIRO) without any financial examination.[153] With a total asset of all Islamic banks, which is estimated according to latest figures between 200

Takaful and Financial Planning. Indiana, p. 23. (Hereafter referred to as Rosly 2005.)

[151] See Warde 2000, p.77.

[152] The Qur'an also provides an appropriate basis in Sura 2, verse 271: „if you show the charities openly, so is it good. If you keep it secret and let it to the poor, it is even better for you, and He will atone for some of your misdeeds. God is aware of what you are doing."

[153] See Brisard, Jean-Charles/Dasquie, Guillaume (2003): Die verbotene Wahrheit: Die Verstrickungen der USA mit Osama bin Laden, Hamburg, pp. 101. (Hereafter referred to as Brisard/Dasquie 2003.)

and 500 billion USD, this kind of "destruction of evidences" might not be without importance.[154]

Meanwhile, there are more than 250 Islamic financial institutions in over 50 countries.[155] Given this abundance of Islamic enterprises, in which business relationships to correspondent banks or shareholdings of other banks are not included, it is virtually impossible to elaborate at this point on any cross-linking of all Islamic banks which are on suspicion of supporting the international terrorism financially.[156] For this reason, the following embodiments will be limited to two banks of Islamic origin, which are exemplary for the practise of an active funding terrorism.

In the wake of the investigations of the financing of the attacks of 9/11, particularly two groups of companies came into the authorities' focus. This concerned the by the naturalized Italian and Egypt-born Youssef Nada[157] controlled a-Taqwa ("Fear of God") and the by the Somali Sheikh Ahmed Nur Jimale founded al-Barakaat (not to be confused with Dallah al-Baraka).[158] The al-Taqwa was established in the 1980s by leaders of the Muslim Brotherhood to give devout Muslims the opportunity to invest their money in accordance with the Qur'an. The bank followed precisely the concept of profit-and-loss sharing modelled on other Islamic financial houses, which circumvented interest rate behaviour as depositors occurred as long term investors. One unusual aspect here was that the bank had no offices, but it

---

[154] See Khan, Nadim/ Mohammed Paracha (2005): No Shortage of Interest. In: The Lawyer 21 March 2005, p. 19.

[155] See ibid.

[156] A complete list of all entities and natural individuals whose assets are frozen either by the US Treasury or blocked by local authorities in cooperating countries is available at the Office of Foreign Asset Control and comprises 179 pages.

[157] Nada himself was a member of the Muslim Brotherhood and was already in the board of the Egyptian Faisal Islamic Bank in the 1970s. See Soliman 2004, p. 273.

[158] See Levitt, Matthew (2002): Charitable and Humanitarian Organizations in the Network of International Terrorist Financing: Testimony before the United States Subcommittee on International Trade and Finance, 1 August 2002.

operated from a small apartment in the Swiss Lugano with four employees. The company was licensed in the Bahamas, which gave it the character of an off-shore bank that was able to correspond with established banks in Europe.[159] In 2001, the bank lost its license in the Bahamas, was liquidated and cancelled from the commercial register. After the Swiss Federal Banking Commission realized in the same year that a branch of al-Taqwa in Lugano perceived no bank-like and thus requiring a special permit, it had to be renamed as Nada Management Organization.[160] In November 2001, Youssef Nade was identified as a financier of Islamic terrorism by the United Nations.[161] Nevertheless, in January 2003 he succeeded travelling to Liechtenstein in order to change the names of two companies that were to be included on the UN list of terror sponsors.[162] Second head of the former al-Taqwa was Ghaleb Himmat who had delicate connections to charitable organizations: From 1973 to 2002 he was chairman of the Islamic Community in Germany, the largest Germany-based group of the Egyptian Muslim Brotherhood in Munich,[163] and he was a board member of the Geneva branch of the Kuwaiti International Islamic Charitable Organization.[164] In a similar manner acted the Somali al-Barakaat: A main component of the legal business were remittances from expatriate Somalis. A part of the fees is said to have arrived directly or indirectly to terrorist organizations through charities.[165] Besides legal generation of money, the al-

---

[159] See Hosenball, Mark (2002): Terror's Cash Flow. In: Newsweek Vol. 139, 25 March 2002, p. 28.

[160] See „Weitere Konten eingefroren". In: Frankfurter Allgemeine Zeitung, 9 November 2001, p. 7.

[161] See Huband, Mark (2001): Bankrolling bin Laden. In: Financial Times, 28 November 2001
(http://specials.ft.com/attackonterrorism/FT3FJ5RJMUC.html). Visited on 23 March 2005.

[162] See Fleischauer, Jan (2004): Puzzlearbeit im Schattenreich. In: Spiegel Special 2, p. 39.

[163] See Vidino, Lorenzo (2005): The Muslim Brotherhood's Conquest of Europe. In: Middle East Quarterly Winter, p. 26.

[164] See Balzli, Beat (2001): Guter Muslim. In: Der Spiegel 46, p. 110.

[165] See Willman, John (2001): Trail of Terrorist Dollars that Spans the World. In: Financial Times, 29 November 2001

Barakaat provided the also in Germany banned *hawala* trade, which is going to be elaborated more detailed below.

But first a prime focus of the analysis are the Islamic organizations that served as in some cases as front organizations for terrorist groups in the transfer of funds and as a pipeline of donations, and that took advantage of the religious duty of *zakat*.

The Islamic Charity Organizations

The fundraising network of the Islamic relief organizations has been progressed over years. Terror organizations such as the Hamas or the Hezbollah maintain both social institutions and private training camps for future terrorists.[166] This combination is thoroughly intended, because only by means of the social commitment the acquisition of donation funds can be justified. If terror organizations like al-Qaeda do not possess a political legitimation like the Hamas or the Hezbollah do, then they depend on collaboration with charitable organizations, which are actively involved for their part in social projects and which pass the collected donations to the respective terror groups on.

Thereby the Islamic charity foundations accommodated with the historical progress: Originally meant to export the Wahhabite belief, governmental organizations with proselytised nature were founded under the pretext of the Saudi Arabian Muslim World League (which was later amended by private foundations). These were represented on the one hand in western countries and relied on given money of the local Diasporas. On the other hand relief organizations were established in regions, where Muslims felt threatened and/or situated in a "holy war".[167]

(http://specials.ft.com/attackonterrorism/FT3RNR3XMUC.html). Visited on 23 March 2005.

[166] See Rößler, Hans-Christian (2003): Terroristen oder Wohltäter? In: Frankfurter Allgemeine Zeitung, 18 July 2003, p. 6.

[167] See "The Iceberg Beneath the Charity". In: Economist Vol. 366, 15 March 2003, p. 67.

The Beginning of Islamic Charity Organizations

The foundation-stone for the development of Islamic relief organizations was laid in May 1962 to an pan Islamic conference in Mecca by Abdullah bin Saleh al-Obayd created Muslim World League (*rabitat al-alam al-Islami*), which was originally thought as counter balance to Nassers politics of the Pan Arabism.[168] The league was expected to socialize contacts to various religious leaders in- and outside the Arab world as rapidly as possible and aimed primarily at the propagation of the Wahhabism in the Islamic communities around the world. For this purpose the books of the mental pioneers of this Puritan version of Sunni Islam, Ibn Taimiyya (1263-1328) and Ibn Abd al-Wahhab (1703-1792) were given as presents as well as governmental funds were made available for building mosques, for setting up and supporting NGOs.[169] Thus, until 2002 nearly 1,500 mosques along with 210 Islamic centers, 202 universities and approx. 2,000 schools in non-Islamic countries were built.[170] Since the end of conflicts in 1995, solely in Bosnia-Herzegovina over 2,000 Saudi-led projects were put in motion to serve the spreading of the Wahhabism.[171] On an area of roughly 500,000 square km new mosques were built - meanwhile there are 158 of these Islamic places of prayer in the Balkans country. With a total population of approx. 2.3 millions and a rate of Sunni Muslims of 44 per cent, an average of circa 6,000 believers per mosque results.[172] Same applied to regions like Afghanistan and Chechnya: Schools

---

[168] Among others, in 1961 Nasser put the renowned University of Al-Azhar in Cairo under government supervision which was received with indignation by the Islamic world. See Warde 2000, p. 91.

[169] See Coll 2004, p. 26.

[170] See Kaplan, David E./Monica Ekman (2003): The Saudi-Connection. In: U.S. News & World Report Vol. 135, 15 December 2003, p. 19.

[171] See Kraske, Marion (2003): In heiliger Mission. In: Der Spiegel 50, p. 156.

[172] However, this kind of missionary was only moderately successful in Bosnia since in general the Islam is not used as a vehicle for radical ideas in this region. The Bosnian Muslims are more pro-Western and hence they have been relatively immune to the Islamism. See Rüb, Matthias (2002): Fremdkörper aus Saudi-Arabien. In: Frankfurter Allgemeine Zeitung, 25 March 2002, p. 6.

and mosques occurred on the one hand; on the other hand local Islamic movements were financially supported.

With the rising income from the oil export, the funds flowed enormously to the individual welfare organizations, which were directly affiliated with the Muslim World League. In particular, this was much more relevant to the al-Haramain Foundation and the Saudi High Commission. According to an official Saudi source (www.saudinf.com), between 1975 and 1987 a total sum of 48 billion USD, i.e. an average of nearly four billion per year was spent for development assistance. At the end of 2002, this sum had risen to altogether 70 billion USD. In view of these numbers not few experts quite agree that the Saudi dynasty has a crucial portion of establishment of radical-Islamic groups in the Middle East.[173]

At the beginning of the 1980s, besides Palestine most notably Afghanistan rank with those areas, in which Muslims felt extraordinary threatened. The war of the Afghans against the Soviet occupiers was the initial moment for the bizarre relationship between Arab sponsors, the Saudi dynasty and radical-Islamic elements. To perfect the coordination of the Saudi funds, which flowed from diverse sources to Afghanistan at that time, the formation of an "Afghan Service Bureau" (Makhtab al-Khidmat) was decided on instruction of the Saudi Red Crescent; its management took on the Jordan Palestinian Abdullah Azzam.[174] This one had originally taught at the King Abdel Aziz University in Jiddah. Azzam held close contacts to Abdul Rasul Sayyaf, who had been sent from Saudi Arabia to

---

[173] „[...]without the exorbitant sums of Saudi money spent on supporting extremist networks and activities, the terrorist threat the world faces today, would roughly be as acute as it is now." See Alexiev, Alex (2004): Ölmilliarden für den Dschihad. In: Internationale Politik 2, p. 23.

[174] Second major recruitment office was the al-Kifah Center in Peshawar which maintained a large number of offices outside Pakistan and Afghanistan. In the United States, connections of the bombers of the World Trade Center in February 1993 to the al-Kifah Center in Brooklyn were proven. This institution received money primarily from the "Afghan Bureau" in Pakistan. See Clarke 2004, p. 113.

Afghanistan in order to agitate the Wahhabism.[175] In a short time, Osama bin Laden gained promotion to Azzams deputy and financial manager since he had bought himself into the "bureau" with an appropriate capital contribution. From this moment, bin Laden established the fundraising in the mosques in order to canvass for the war against Soviet occupying forces in Afghanistan.[176]

From then on, Makhtab al-Khidmat started to emerge to a central collecting point for Saudi donations likewise the Saudi government had actually imagined. This was where all funds of the Saudi secret service Istakhbarat,[177] the Saudi Red Crescent, the Muslim World League and Saudi mosques gathered.[178] At the very same time, it conduced as a place of assembly for the new recruits who joined the jihad against the Red Army from outside of Afghanistan – the so-called Arab Afghans.[179]

Numerous persons, who were later linked to assaults in East Africa, India, Pakistan, Egypt and the US, took an active part in the war in Afghanistan. Thus, bin Ladens today's consultant and physician, Ayman al-Zawahiri worked for the Saudi Red Crescent back then when the two terror tycoons met the first time in

---

[175] See Scheuer 2003, pp. 274.

[176] See Hermann, Rainer (2001): Der Terrorist und sein Finanznetz. In: Frankfurter Allgemeine Zeitung, 29 September 2001, p. 15.

[177] Head of the Saudi intelligence then was Prince Turki bin Faisal, who had resigned his office a few days before the 9/11 attacks and who is now representing his country as ambassador in London since 2003. Of all member of the Saudi royal family al-Saud, he was the strongest advocate of Taliban interests on the Arabian Peninsula. On one of his meetings with Afghan religious students in June 1998 and in presence of senior al-Qaeda commanders, he is said to have renounced an extradition of bin Laden to Riyadh if Saudi Arabia is going to be spared terrorist attacks in future. In addition, to the one-eyed Taliban leader Mullah Omar Akhund grants were promised. See Interview with Turki Ibn al-Faisal Al Saud (2004). In: Der Spiegel 11, p. 119.

[178] See Thamm, Berndt Georg (2002): Kaderschmiede des islamistischen Privatterrorismus. In: Politische Studien 381, Vol. 53, p. 58. (Hereafter referred to as Thamm 2002.)

[179] See Rashid, Ahmed: Taliban (2001): Die afghanischen Gotteskrieger und der Dschihad. Munich, p. 225. (Hereafter referred to as Rashid 2001.)

1985.[180] Also active for the Red Crescent was Wa'el Hamza Jalaidan who administers the Muslim World League office in Pakistan simultaneously.[181] On September 6, 2002, the US Treasury put him on a list of terror sponsors.[182] According to newspaper data, the US administration feels quite certain to claim: The Saudi businessman from Jeddah is the logistical head and co-founder of al-Qaeda.[183]

The Functioning of Islamic Relief Organizations before September 11, 2001

Likewise terrorism expert Matthew Levitt determined, the financial backers remained the same persons over years that did not depend their donations on a single organization but on their objectives and actions.[184] If attacks are to be observed, then they function to the highest degree as a marketing concept for the sponsors of terrorism – without any specific political action the capital flow peters out.

A lot of charity organizations that worked under the banner of Islam, served in the past the terrorists for generating money in terms of money acquisition or veiling of money transfer. Although the investigations in the course of the bombings in New York 1993 and East Africa revealed clear connections of the terrorists to numerous Islamic relief organizations, precious

---

[180] See Valdmanis, Thor (2001): Family, Friends Tell of the Man Behind bin Laden. In: USA Today, 12 October 2001, p. A13.
[181] See Emerson, Steven (2003): Terrorism Financing: Origination, Organization, and Prevention. Saudi Arabia, Terrorist Financing and the War on Terror. Testimony before the United States Senate Committee on Governmental Affairs, 31 July 2003, p. 18.
[182] See Department of the Treasury (2002): Treasury Department Statement on the Designation of Wa'el Hamza Julidan, Press Release, 6 September 2002.
[183] See "Funds Continue to Flow Despite Drive to Freeze Network's Assets". In: The Guardian, 5 September 2002 (http://www.guardian.co.uk/international/story/0,,786103,00.html#article_contin ue). Visited on 4 November 2004.
[184] See Grossbongardt, Anette (2004): Die Millionen der Hamas.In: Spiegel Special 2, p. 102.

little actions were taken.[185] It was only the devastating attacks of the September 11, 2001 caused the US officials to take forceful steps against financial resources of the Islamist terrorists. Quite fast it became apparent how Islamic charity organizations, apparently legally working covert companies, according to Islamic law working banks (including their correspondent banks), financially potent private persons and radical-Islamic groups correlated.

Organizations with charitable claims presented a special temptation for the most diverse reasons to radical-Islamic groups. Primarily, the collected donations of *zakat* were directly passed on the specific relief organizations. On the other hand, it is in the nature of things that charitable institutions are operative in regions where civil wars or other forms of conflicts are present. This enables them to be close to the planning centre of the terrorists. Thirdly, Islamic relief organizations do not only serve the generating of funds, but besides they are suitable for transferring appropriate assets unnoticed by authorities.[186] In other words, whenever funds are sent to trouble areas, misuse or proper application cannot be distinguished at the beginning of the transfer.[187]

This is one of the largest problems for the prevention of misusing donations by terrorists and their affiliates: Islamic charity organizations which are under suspicion of financing terrorism, hardly ever used the entire funds in the past to maintenance training camps. Constantly they pursued a two-pronged policy and merged their contact to radical-Islamic groups with familiar philanthropic work, e.g. with the

---

[185] See Vistica, Gregory L./ Daniel Klaidman (1998): Tracking Terror. In: Newsweek Vol. 132, 19 October 1998, pp. 46.

[186] See Sachs, Susan (2001): An Investigation in Egypt Illustrates Al Qaeda's Web. In: New York Times, 21 November 2001, p. A1.

[187] See "The Iceberg Beneath the Charity" In: Economist Vol. 366, 15 March 2003, p. 67.

construction of schools and hospitals.[188] So after the Taliban had banished western organizations, only accredited ones were locally active. Islamic organizations adopted mostly the supply of the country and its important regions such as of the capital Kabul or Kandahar thereby, whereas the Taliban in general did not bother about what happened to their subjects. For example, the Islamic Al Rashid Trust stated that it was responsible for the feeding of approx. 300,000 humans in Afghanistan.[189]

As it later discovered, the Al Rashid Trust was one of the most radical so-called relief organizations. The Al Rashid Trust was closely connected to the terrorist group of Jaish-e-Mohammed (successor organization of Harakat al-Mudschaheddin) whose religious leader and founder, Maulana Masood Azhar had been obtained released from prison after a plane hi-jacking of the Indian airline flight IC-814 in exchange for 178 hostages in December 1999. During the takeover of the plane the hi-jackers used a similar method like the death pilots on September 11, 2001 did: as a deterrent they cut a passenger's throat while his wife had to watch him bleeding to excess.[190] Furthermore, the Al Rashid Trust is under strong suspicion of being involved in the kidnapping and killing of the US journalist Daniel Pearl. Because the hut in Karachi in which Pearl was kept imprisoned, was property of the Al Rashid Trust.[191]

---

[188] Both, Hamas and Hezbollah guarantee social benefits in the form of medical care and school attendances to their supporters. Especially the social sector mirrors the traditions of the Muslim Brotherhood. Founded in 1928 by the Egyptian Hassan al-Banna, the Muslim Brotherhood considered its mission to participate heavily in education and welfare activities. That included, among others, the construction and maintenance of hospitals, feeding the poor and needy, and the establishment of evening schools to combat illiteracy and to teach the Qur'an. See Laqueur, Walter (2001): Die globale Bedrohung: Neue Gefahren des Terrorismus, Munich, pp. 177-182.
[189] See Cohen, Laurie P. et. al (2001): Bush's Financial War on Terrorism Includes Strikes on Islamic Charities. In: Wall Street Journal, 25 September 2001, p. A1.
[190] See Rao, Padma et. al (2001): "Wir dachten, nun ist alles aus". In: Der Spiegel 2, pp. 126.
[191] See Levitt, Matthew (2002): The Political Economy of Middle East Terrorism. In: Middle East Review of International Affair Vol. 6, No. 4, p. 57.

In General, the attention to the charitable organizations and their defamation as terror financier was notably for US officials a delicate topic because the investigations about the origins of the funds or their misuse led almost always to the same sender – Saudi Arabia and therewith straight to the own current history of the USA. Until the attacks of New York, Washington and Pennsylvania this kind of inquiries was not quite popular in the USA. Before then, hints were neglected, which led in any way to the Arab peninsula and could possibly discredit a member of the Saudi royal family.[192] For reasons of political convenience, an excessively stressed sensitivity and the desire for protecting the US-Saudi relationship, at least some sections of the US administration felt anxious not to pursue much further the becoming increasingly obvious Saudi support of terrorists. And of course a decisive factor in this was considerations in terms of energy policy that the origins of the terror funds did not become public after the USA had decided for the way of "pedro-industrial syndrome", as Michael Ehrke characterized.[193]

The openly defined suspicion towards Saudi officials after September 11, 2001 was by no means a coincidence and got them into argumentation troubles because surprisingly the Saudi government avoided cutting back its connections to dubious relief organizations. For example it was common, that organizations such as the IIRO or the al-Haramain were allowed to use rooms inside the Saudi embassy unless they were not equipped with own offices in the respective country.[194] This led among other things to an embarrassing incident in 2001: After the invasion of the northern alliance under general Daud on November 13, employees of the Saudi embassy were arrested

---

[192] See Napoleoni 2004, p. 42.

[193] "The over many decades guaranteed supply of Western economies with cheap oil has created a de facto subsidized 'petro-industrial complex' (from the oil industry to the automotive) which relies on a continuous flow of cheap oil, and which is politically strong enough to influence goverment policy of the Western democracy."See Ehrke, Michael (2003): Erdöl und Strategie: Zur politischen Ökonomie eines angekündigten Krieges. In: Internationale Politik und Gesellschaft 1, pp. 13.

[194] See ibid. p. 24.

who worked for the al-Haramain Foundation as later turned out. The manager of the Afghan branch, Nasser bin Mohammed al Gilale, put on record in the following hearing, he was instructed by Riyadh to provide furthermore for Saudi nationals who were still in the hard-fought Afghanistan. However, since Saudi Arabia had officially broken off diplomatic relations to the Taliban and had closed the embassy in Kabul on September 25, which roughly meant: The al-Haramain Foundation had been authorized by highest officials to care for the Saudi contingent of al-Qaeda.[195] Naturally these accusations were dismissed by the Saudi Interior Secretary literally as "rubbish": al-Haramain is a "charitable association whose goal is solely to help needy humans".[196]

Al-Haramain was either formed in 1992 by the Saudi Secretary of Religion Saleh bin Abdulaziz al-Sheikh[197] or four years before by Akil al-Akil in Pakistan.[198] Financially the foundation was closely tied to the Saudi financial group Dallah al-Baraka whose founder and majority shareholder is Saleh Abdullah Kamel. Akil al-Akil remained as directing manager of the foundation until 2003 and had an entry as co-owner of the al-Nur mosque in Berlin.[199] Since its formation the foundation was present in those regions where Muslims fought out their "holy war": in Afghanistan,

---

[195] See Ulfkotte, Udo (2001): Treibt Riad ein doppeltes Spiel? In: Frankfurter Allgemeine Zeitung, 5 December 2001, p. 6.

[196] See Interview with Prince Naif (2001). In: Der Spiegel 51, p. 160.

[197] See Dohnanyi, Johannes und Germana (2002): Schmutzige Geschäfte und Heiliger Krieg: Al-Qaida in Europa. Munich, p. 225. (Hereafter referred to as Dohnanyi 2002.)

[198] See Kocher, Viktor (2004): Saudisches Hilfswerk unter Anklage. In: Neue Zürcher Zeitung, 13 October 2004
(http://www.nzz.ch/dossiers/2003/terrorismus/2004.10.13-al-article9X2GH.html). Visited on 2 November 2004.

[199] The costs oft he mosque, just the property had a value of about 2.3 million D-Mark, were payed to 75 percent by the al-Haramain Foundation. For purchasing this property someone else was responsible. A person named Mohammed Fakihi worked at the Saudi embassy in Berlin and was accredited as an attaché. Inter alia he is supposed to have met with a prime suspect of the Hamburg terrorist cell, Motassadeq in the Hamburg mosque al-Quds after the attacks of 9/11. See Mascolo, Georg (2003): Die Saudi-Connection. In: Der Spiegel 14, p. 72.

Somalia, Bosnia, Kenya, Pakistan and Chechnya.[200] Already in February 2002, branches of the al-Haramain Foundation in Bosnia and Somalia were officially denounced by US authorities as a supporting organ of terrorism and imposed sanctions against it, i.e. its banking accounts and assets were frozen.[201]

At the latest since the trial against the assassins of the 1998 bombings in East Africa, starting in February 2001, the al-Haramain was no longer unknown to US authorities.[202] Amazingly, the foundation could nevertheless continue to operate and provide terrorist with money, and its branches in the USA in Ashland/Oregon and Springfield/Missouri only were put on a list of terror sponsors on September 9, 2004 after the US administration had requested the financial sector to freeze respective assets of the foundation.[203] And so, within a month, the al-Haramain was terminated by the Saudi government and thereby this can be considered as a quite successful example in the war against financing terrorism. After the demission of Akil in 2003, the foundation came under the authority of the Saudi Department of Islamic Affairs before it was completely liquidated and its roughly 5,000 employees were laid off on October 5, 2004, right after the US pressure had risen and the foundation had become incapable of acting due to its frozen assets.[204] Akil al-Akil was classified as terror sponsor by US

---

[200] See Stein, Lisa: Charity or Front? In: U.S. News & World Report Vol. 136, 2 February 2004, p. 14.
[201] See Stark, Holger: Großzügige Gaben. In: Der Spiegel 32, p. 30.
[202] See „Synchrone Anschläge". In: Frankfurter Allgemeine Zeitung, 24 September 2001, p. 9.
[203] See Aversa, Jeannine: Bush Administration Accuses Saudi Charity of Financing Terrorism. In: Associated Press, 9 September 2004.
[204] See "Saudis Shut Down Charity". In: Al Jazeera Online, 5 October 2004 (http://english.aljazeera.net/NR/exeres/E358AE91-FAEC-407C-BDE9-31E80C0BA37B.htm). Visited on 2 November 2004.

authorities on June 2, 2004.[205] So far, legal measures against him are not been taken in Saudi Arabia.[206]

According to the by now erased internet presence www.alharamain.org, the foundation collected between 45 and 50 million USD a year, and spent in total about 300 million USD for philanthropic programs world-wide. These included the construction of mosques and the establishment of Muslim schools. A link to radical-Islamic elements was always denied.[207]

Second considerable charity organization was the International Islamic Relief Organization (IIRO), which was directly associated to the Muslim World League. The IIRO was founded in 1978 and had its head office in Jeddah.[208] The IIRO can be viewed as one of the financial main branches of the Muslim World League. It got involved in Bosnia-Herzegovina as one of the first relief organizations. Quite fast connections to local radical-Islamic groups were made, so that the IIRO had to quit working in the Balkans country.[209] The same applied to the attacks in Kenya and Tanzania in 1998. The following investigations revealed a detailed image of the apparently charitable working organization. Besides the supply of money and other logistics, instructions for terrorist attacks were given allegedly by the relief organizations, i.e. it had close contacts to the highest command level of al-Qaeda.

---

[205] See US-Department of the Treasury (2004): Additional Al Haramain Branches, Former Leader Designated by Treasury as al Qaeda Supporters: Treasury Marks Latest Actions in Joint Designation with Saudi Arabia, Press Release, 2 June 2004.

[206] See Comras, Victor (2005): Al Qaeda Finances and Funding to Affiliated Groups. In: Strategic Insights Vol. IV, Issue I, January 2005, p. 5. (Hereafter referred to as Comras 2005.)

[207] See Kestenholz, Daniel (2003): Saudisches Geld für indonesische Terroristen? In: Die Welt, 15 July 2003
(http://www.welt.de/data/2003/07/15/133989.html?prx=1). Visited on 3 December 2004.

[208] See Brisard/Dasquie 2003, p. 96.

[209] See ibid. p. 97.

Right after the Washington had felt obliged to respond the attacks in East Africa by bombing a chemical plant in Sudan and a training camp in Afghanistan, the Indian police arrested a number of suspected individuals who were planning assaults on US consulates in Madras and Calcutta. The terror cell was managed by a Bengali named Sayed Abu Nasir who had received commands from Shaykh Ahmed al-Gamdin, the managing director of the Asian IIRO, according to his own statements. Nasir worked for the IIRO after he had graduated college in his homeland, and he finally arrived to Lahore in Pakistan via Thailand. Abu Nasir got insight into the working methods of the organization: approx. 40 to 50 per cent of the annual budget was straight passed on to training camps of terrorists in Afghanistan and Kashmir. Nasir's task was among others to inspect the camps and to notice their needs as well as to compose reports which were sent to the head quarter in Jeddah. During this activity he probably himself forward for higher objectives. He received order from al-Gamdin to gain military training in one of the training camps. There, he presumptively was in contact with Osama bin Laden.[210]

Bin Laden's brother-in-law, Mohammed Jamal Khalifa worked for the IIRO from 1986 to 1994 as well and managed the office of the organization on the Philippines from which he channelled Saudi Arabia originated funds to al-Qaeda.[211] Likewise local groups such as the Philippine Abu Sayyaf ("Carrier of the Sword") were supported, which were primarily financed by ransom businesses, and among others it received 20 million USD for the Sipadan hostages in 2000.[212] Years later, after Khalifa had left the office, the Philippine branch of the IIRO became a crucial point of Saudi donations. In 1999, the Saudi government

---

[210] See Emerson, Steven (2003): Terrorism Financing. Origination, Organization, and Prevention. Saudi Arabia, Terrorist Financing, and the War on Terror: Testimony before the United States Committee on Governmental Affairs, 31 July 2003, p. 20.
[211] See Gunaratna 2003, p. 242.
[212] See Kremp, Jürgen (2001): Gewalt gegen Gewalt. In: Der Spiegel 23, p. 154.

discovered that the head of the National Commercial Bank, Khalid bin Machfus had transferred approx. three million USD to institutions which were already at that time suspected to donor bin Laden with money.[213] Thereby, the funds originated from financially extremely potent businessmen in Saudi Arabia who had a total fortune of nearly five billion USD. Through banks in New York and London, a part of the money is said to be eventually arrived to IIRO. The other two foundations were called Islamic Relief and Blessed Relief, also known by its Arabic name Muwafak.[214] Its chairman Yasin al-Qadi, a Jeddah-based businessman, was classified by the United States as terrorist financier on October 12, 2001.[215]

Despite all endeavours by the today's Secretary-General of the IIRO Adnan bin Khalil Pasha to free the organization of the suspicion of financing terrorism, the backing by means of donations seems to continue – only the recipient became another one: In place of al-Qaeda, now the Hamas has apparently gotten highest priority and obtains funds chiefly from the Arab region.[216]

---

[213] The family of bin Mahfourz is in addition to the bin Laden family, one of the most influential businessmen of Saudi Arabia. Jointly with the family of al-Amuidi they own the Delta Oil Corporation which established with the Californian-based Unocal the CentGas Consortium for the pipeline project in Afghanistan..See Rashid 2001, p. 287.
[214] See Kelley, Jack (1999): Saudi Money Aiding bin Laden. In: USA Today, 29 October 1999, p. A1.
[215] See US-Department of the Treasury (2001): Treasury Department Releases List of 39 Additional Specially Designated Global Terrorists, Press Release, 12 October 2001.
[216] See Stalinsky, Steven: Saudi Royal Family's Financial Support to the Palestinians 1998-2003: More than 15 Billion Riyals ($4 Billion U.S.) given to 'Mujahideen Fighters' and 'Families of Martyrs'. In: Middle East Media Research Institute, Special Report No. 17
(http://memri.org/bin/opener.cgi?Page=archives&ID=SR1703). Visited on 30 July 2004.

The Functioning of Islamic Relief Organizations after September 11, 2001

In general, the efforts of the administrative bodies in the course of the 9/11 attacks and the following pursuit of their financiers seem to have had little consequences for the finances of al-Qaeda – at least this applies on the group of private donors. A report of the UN Monitoring Group stated on August 22, 2002, even after almost one year after 9/11, the al-Qaeda can still rely on donations of private individuals amounting to 16 million USD per annum.[217] These figures correspond approximately to the monthly income of the al-Qaeda ranging between one and two million USD, estimated by the Canadian secret service.[218]

The private donors, however, are only one side of the medal. In the decade before September 11, 2001, the Saudi government alone spent about ten billion USD to Islamic welfare organizations.[219] What ever happened to these dollars, where these were invested or into what hands they were given – obviously this was never part of an analysis. An income tax system, equivalent to Western standards, does not exist in the Arab hemisphere. Hence, there is no fiscal authority that fixes the *zakat* transfers in writing. Once transacted payments cannot be traced back.[220] Private individuals, who move grand-scale amounts to the respective organizations, benefit from this system.

Paying the *zakat* or the *saddaqah* is a very personal obligation. Donations are expected to help suffering people, to bolster

---

[217] See Second Report of the Monitoring Group Established Pursuant to Security Council Resolution 1363 (2001) and Extended by Resolution 1390 (2002), S/2002/1050, 20 September 2002, p. 11.
[218] See Zuckerman, Mortimer B. (2002): Who Finances the Fanatics? In: U.S. News & World Report Vol. 133, 30 December 2002, p. 92.
[219] See Shahar, Yael (2001): Tracing bin Laden's Money: Easier Said than Done, Institute for CounterTerrorism, 21 September 2001
(http://www.ict.org.il/articles/articledet.cfm?articleid=387). Visited on 4 October 2004.
[220] See Comras 2005, p. 3.

orphans or for instance to enable the construction of schools, so the initial thought tells. For that purpose the *zakat* funds were usually amassed on behalf of the Saudi government resp. the Department of Islamic Affairs. In addition, in whole Saudi Arabia so-called donation boxes were installed mostly outside of supermarkets or shops in which money could be thrown in. In 2003 these containers were abolished by law of the Saudi government.[221] And on February 28, 2004, King Fahd created a central agency for relief work abroad therewith the donation campaigns of the approx. 300 Saudi organizations could be monitored.[222]

Meanwhile, the efficiency of such measures seems to be limited: Reports about the financial support of terrorist groups in Iraq have delivered whereupon terrorists rely on the same financial structure as the al-Qaeda did in the past. Essential elements are: charitable institutions, front companies and a significant amount of cash money from Saudi Arabia[223] and other Arab countries.[224] So the mentioned tendency seems to be confirmed: May the terrorist groups change, the financial backers stay the same.

Apparent Legal Business

In August 2002 a report of the UN Monitoring Group stated that bin Laden and his al-Qaeda further dispose of apparently legal investments. The portfolio of these enterprises is said to lie between 30 and 300 million USD.[225] Sums like these can only be

---

[221] See Raphaeli, Nimrod (2003): Financing of Terrorism: Sources, Methods, and Channels. In: Terrorism and Political Violence Vol. 15, No. 4, p. 78.

[222] See "Saudis Shut Down Charity". In: Al Jazeera Online, 5 October 2004 (http://english.aljazeera.net/NR/exeres/E358AE91-FAEC-407C-BDE9-31E80C0BA37B.htm). Visited on 2 November 2004.

[223] See Lumpkin, John J. (2004): Insurgents Infiltrating Iraq Have Cash. In: Associated Press, 21 October 2004.

[224] See US-Department of the Treasury (2005): Al-Zarkawi Financier Designated by the Treasury, Press Release, 13 April 2005.

[225] See Second Report of the Monitoring Group Established Pursuant to Security Council Resolution 1363 (2001) and Extended by Resolution 1390 (2002), S/2002/1050. 20 September 2002, p. 11.

roughly estimated. It is, however, unlikely that terror organizations such as Hamas or al-Qaeda defray their annual budget for the most part by using apparent legal businesses. In fact, such businesses existed in the past – while its economic value rather negligible. But this kind of businesses seems to have served a different purpose.

The trial against the assassins of Nairobi, Kenya and Daressalam, Tanzania at the district court of the state of New York provided to the US authorities a detailed insight into genesis of the former Saudi national bin Laden. The witness for the prosecution, Jamaal al-Fadl, first-generation member of al-Qaeda, declared in his testimony of his time in Sudan.

When bin Laden visited the Sudan for the first time in 1990 and completely re-located to Khartoum in 1992, and so the operational base of al-Qaeda was transferred, a series of fronts were established respectively company share were bought.[226] In 1990, bin Laden handed over about two million USD to the Sudanese leader of the Islamic Party (National Islamic Front, Defaa
al-Shabi), Hassan al-Turabi, for the return of the "Arab Afghans" to Sudan as well as another 10.5 million USD for the moderinization of the Sudanese flour industry and for the construction of an airport near Port Sudan. Personally, bin Laden bought into the newly founded al_Shamal Bank ("Bank of the North") and acquired shares amounting to 50 million USD.[227]

This was just the beginning. In 1992, the entire cadre of al-Qaeda was re-located from Afghanistan to Sudan. Al-Fadl functioned thereby as a vanguard who had to rent or buy farms, accommodations and offices. According to his own statements,

---

[226] See Herrmann, Frank (1996): Osama bin Laden – der Bankier des Terrors. In: Berliner Zeitung, 28 October 1996, p. 6.
[227] See Scheuer 2003, pp. 122.

two-thirds of these farms were conceived as training camps. The rest should intend the cultivation of agricultural products.[228]

Apparently, al-Qaeda possessed all the needed liberties in Sudan and it was totally shielded by the Sudanese secret service. Al-Fadl or Abu Bakr al-Sudani, his then pseudonym, was during his activity for the al-Qaeda fitted with strong legal powers which allowed him for example to cross customs barriers.[229] So that meant that commodities or container, addressed to the newly founded al-Qaeda front Wadi al-Aqiq Company and imported into the Sudan, did not become scanned.

Since that time, starting from 1991, the Wadi al-Aqiq functioned as some kind of holding company for future formation of al-Qaeda fronts. These included the Ladin International Company, Taba Investments, Hijra Constructions (a building firm responsible for the construction of the so-called revolution road from Khartoum to Port Sudan), Al-Themar al-Mubaraka, al-Qudurat Transportation and a fruit and vegetable company of unknown name.[230]

Main exports goods of the Ladin International and the Themar al-Mubaraka were among others leathers, sesame, honey, peanuts, wheat and the internationally desired Gum Arabic.[231] But the key factor was that at the end of 1991 a terrorist cell came into being which could perform its job undisturbed of any

---

[228] See United States of America vs. Usama bin Laden, et al. United States District Court, Southern District of New York, 6 February 2001, p. 220.

[229] See ibid. p. 239.

[230] See Müller, Tilmann (1998): Die Terror GmbH. In: Stern 41, p. 48.

[231] Gum Arabic is an already hardened latex of the North African gum acacias. It serves to produce glue and water colours. Above all, it is indispensable in the production of caffeinated soft drinks: Without Gum Arabic, the fruit content drops at the bottom of the bottles. The United States get their Gum Arabic exclusively from the Sudan, where about 80 percent of the world production comes from. For the managers of Coca-Cola and Pepsi, the latex conveys a similar fundamental meaning like oil for the world trade. After all, their product stands like no other for the realization of the American lifestyle. See Duran, Khalid (1998): Geschäfte mit dem großen Satan. In: Frankfurter Allgemeine Zeitung, 26 May 1998, p. 10.

effects from in- and outside of Sudan. It seems likely that al-Qaeda became thanks to the Sudanese stage to the network we know today.

From his office in the McNimr Street in Khartoum, bin Laden gave his full support to Islamic movements in- and outside of the Arab hemisphere. With this in mind, al-Fadl embarked on a journey to Kenya,[232] Hungary[233] and Jordan[234] – in each case he was equipped with cash that was passed to local contacts.

It is assumed that the yields of the Sudanese companies were barely enough to compensate the employees and the al-Qaeda members – thus for the day-to-day management. From a financial point of view, the Sudanese episode remained to bin Laden as a veritable disaster: When he was forced to leave the country under the pressure of the USA and Egypt in 1998, approx, bin Laden suffered losses amounting 150 million USD and his companies were confiscated.[235] Structurally considered, he had established the al-Qaeda.

Currently, it is to be expected that terror oriented organizations with a global range, e.g. the Hezbollah or al-Qaeda, only a fractional amount of their annual budget is generated through legally working companies.[236] The bulk of the yearly income is carried by the mentioned donations of individuals and the *zakat* transfer of Diasporas by means of charitable institutions.

---

[232] See United States of America vs. Usama bin Laden, et al. United States District Court, Southern District of New York, 6 February 2001, p. 309.

[233] See ibid. p. 313.

[234] See ibid. p. 317.

[235] See O'Harrow, Robert et al. (2001): Bin Laden's Money Takes Hidden Paths To Agents of Terror. In: Washington Post, 21 September 2001, p. A13.

[236] Friedrich Schneider estimates, according to his own calculations, the proportion of illegally acquired funds through front companies to about ten percent of the total income of al-Qaeda. See Schneider, Friedrich: Die Finanzströme islamischer Terror-Organisationen. Vorläufige Erkenntnisse aus volkswirtschaftlicher Sicht (Written version of an invited presentation at the symposium „Money Laundering and Covert Terrorist Financing. Threat to the Community of States", organized by the German Federal Intelligence Service). Pullach, 25 October 2001, p. 25.

In July 2004, the 9/11 commission report, which dealt with the background of the attacks of September 11, 2001, came to the conclusion that bin Laden received support on a large scale from the Gulf region, and he could rely less on his private fortune than so far anticipated.[237] Furthermore, the report emphasized that al-Qaeda and in particular its single cells around the globe are funded by small-scale crime, which will be discussed in the next chapter.[238]

---

[237] See National Commission on Terrorist Attacks Upon the United States (2004): The 9/11 Commission Report. New York,p. 170.
[238] See ibid. p. 171.

5 FINANCING TERRORISM FROM ILLEGAL SOURCES

In the decades before the September 11, 2001, the phenomena of organized crime and terrorism were handled separately.[239] Although both representing groups had similar methods, but their goals differed from each other: "Criminals and terrorists manipulate money in somewhat different ways organized criminal activity is motivated by simple profit - amassing staggering sums either legally or illegally. For terrorists groups, though, the money (amassed however) is a means to other ends".[240] Different objectives, however, did not prevent cooperation between terrorism and organized crime in the past. In this respect, there were enough points of contact, which affected to be profitable for both parties. At present, this

---

[239] Consistently the Clinton administration rated political violence as a criminal act and not as an act of national threat. This view changed with the incidents of 9/11: Terrorism was no longer a criminal offense but rather considered as an act o war. See Napoleoni 2004, pp. 39-42. See also Andreas, Peter/Richard Price (2001): From War Fighting to Crime Fighting: Transforming the American National Security State. In: International Studies Review Vol. 3, pp.36.
[240] See Thachuk, Kimberley L. (2002): Terrorism's Financial Lifeline: Can It be Severed? In: Strategic Forum. Institute for National Strategic Studies National Defense University No. 191, p. 3. (Hereafter referred to as Thachuk 2002.)

symbiosis is particularly evident in the Colombian Fuerzas Armadas Revolucionarias de Colombia (FARC) where the two groups converged to almost indistinguishability.[241] Terrorist activities fade as such and are only for the protection of their own sphere of influence: in this case, the cultivation fields of the coca plant.

A separation of both terms seems at this stage no longer useful. As Udo Ulfkotte stated, "Terrorism and organized crime, [...] more or less 'identical twins'",[242] which sometimes have similar structures: they each have a logistical and a (Para-) military wing with special tasks. They are funded via the same channels, use the same smuggling routes and both need counterfeit documents to transfer internationally. The cooperation becomes visible on the basis of preparation of terrorist activities: arms dealers profit from the sale of their goods to terrorist-oriented groups, which would be without these logistical supplies less powerful, traffickers in human being provide terrorists with escape routes to their sanctuaries; money launderers and money couriers ensure the execution of actions.

For quite some time, the US intelligence hypothesises that in future we will watch a building relationship between the groups of terrorism and the organized crime. In late 2000, the US National Intelligence Council prepared a study that highlighted various threat scenarios. Above all, the report specified at that time the ideal fertile soil on which both groups could grow and prosper: "They will form loose alliances with one another, with small criminal entrepreneurs, and with insurgent movements for specific operations. They will corrupt leaders oft unstable, economically fragile or failing states, insinuate themselves into troubled banks and businesses, and corporate with insurgent political movements to control substantial geographic areas. [...] States with poor governance [...] weak economics and porous

---

[241] See Foxell 2003, pp. 187.
[242] See Ulfkotte, Udo (2003): Der Krieg in unseren Städten: Das geheime Netzwerk der Terroristen. Frankfurt/Main, p. 135.

borders will be prime breeding grounds for terrorism. In such states, domestic groups will challenge the entrenched government, and transnational networks seeking safe havens."[243]

The present terrorist generation works supremely optimized. Cross-connections in the legal sector are much stronger pronounced than this may have applied to the rather ideologically motivated terrorism of the German Red Army Fraction or the Italian Brigate Rosse.[244] Terrorists hold shares of particular companies, own equity funds, and they maintain special links to the international high finance; plus, their balance of payments is equalized. Suicide bombings represent besides their military benefits a financial component even a financial component. Though, the families of the bombers are supported financially, nevertheless, for them no withdrawal plan needs to be created.[245] Moreover, the risk that traces can be possibly backtracked and any financial channels can be closed by administrative bodies, is much lower.

Yet, money remains ambivalent for terrorist-oriented organizations. At one extreme, risen donations enhance the military clout of terrorist groups. They are in a position to bribe authorities, by use of false documents they are able to move freely or they even found fronts to disguise their finances. To much importance is attached to the purchase of arms: with the exception of chemical, biological or nuclear weapons, in so many regions of the world it is an easy matter to enter into possession of firearms – especially since the arsenal of the former Soviet

---

[243] See The National Intelligence Council (2000): Global Trends 2015: A Dialogue About the Future With Nongovernment Experts. Washington, pp. 41, 50.
[244] See Hirschmann 2003, pp. 18.
[245] For Palestinian suicide bombers who blew themselves up against Israeli targets, the remaining relatives received grants up to 25,000 USD either from Iran, Iraq or other Arab countries. But those who were killed in military action against Israel, were only worth 6,000 USD. See Laqueur, Walter (2004): Krieg dem Westen: Terrorismus im 21. Jahrhundert. Berlin, p. 138.

Union opened for a long time.[246] Primarily, money offers security in planning to a group, considering the use of political violence, and this makes the terrorist able to operate for a long-term.

In contrast, there is a different, secular thought: money corrupts people – including terrorists and religious zealots. According to sources associated to the bombers of 9/11, it became known that the group of Mohammed Atta did not afford even the smallest luxury, they kept record for every expenditure, and they even had to transfer surplus cash back to Dubai.[247] The same happened to the Brigate Rosse in Italy during the 1970s[248] and to the Colombian FARC. Because "the higher the revenues of the group from the drug business turned out, the more they depend on thrive of this industry. This in turn depends on the continued existence of the still bribed administration [in Bogota], so in this case it makes little sense to topple the government which created the environment of the own livelihood."[249] A failing or already failed state easily turn out to be a trap for terrorism: As the example of the FARC proved, it is possible that the originally by terrorist targeted state and its corrupted system progress into a partnership – this situation was different when the also Colombian M19 declared the armed struggle has to continue because the encouraged reforms would not progress sufficiently fast.

After the US victory on the Taliban, in association with the coalition forces of operation "Enduring Freedom", al-Qaeda had

---

[246] In this content, the person of Viktor Bout must be named. He reflects a model example for the cooperation between the Islamic terrorism and organized crime. See Winer 2002, p. 25.

[247] See Griffith, Victoria et al.(2001): How the Hijackers Went Unnoticed. In: Financial Times, 29 November 2001
(http://specials.ft.com/attackonterrorism/FT3LAJ6UMUC.html). Visited on 23 May 2005.

[248] In the search of the conspirative apartment where the kidnapping of Aldo Moro has been prepared, the police found bills, that documented even the smallest expenditure of the group: converted 4 € for gas, 8 € for pens etc. See Sterling 1983, p. 391.

[249] See Adams 1990, p. 381.

to undergo a process of transformation. Its structures had been destroyed, numerous senior members of the network were caught and al-Qaeda has been restricted in its maneuverability. And furthermore, it has been decentralized which roughly means that the once created committees of the organization which took for instance the responsibility of the media relations, the exercise of religion, the military training and the control of finances, do not have any influence of any kind on the "holy war".

By now, the al-Qaeda affiliated cells functions as some kind of a franchise company, i.e., instructions from the command centre of terror are no longer necessary for the implementation of upcoming attacks.[250] In this case, al-Qaeda serves mainly as a "ideological reference", according to the Spanish terrorism expert Baltasar Garzon.[251] Recent attacks – after 2001 – are hardly assigned to al-Qaeda itself because in this way it does no longer exist.

Detailed instructions concerning the financial self-sufficiency of individual cells of al-Qaeda were delivered by a manual named "Declaration of Jihad against the Country's Tyrants" fount by the Manchester Metropolitan Police in the year 2000 which was saved on a computer under the same "Military Series."[252] Lesson three dealt with in particular with the counterfeiting of documents and it prescribed the properly handling of the available funds. Basically, the funds had to be split: one part for investments, the other for operational purposes. Furthermore, the security standards mandated how to deal with the operational money. To prevent any future investigations, the whereabouts of the funds should be concealed to lower-ranking members and the group's assets should be not stored in a single place. The investments itself had to be done by persons who were not directly linked to the organizations.[253]

---

[250] See „Vergebliche Warnungen". In: Der Spiegel 42 (2004), p. 107.

[251] See Cziesche, Dominik et al. (2005): "Schwert und Blut". In: Der Spiegel, 28, p. 30.

[252] See Thamm 2002, p. 65.

[253] See Declaration of Jihad Against the Country's Tyrants: Military Series,

In case of any financial support for the affiliated groups on behalf of the al-Qaeda command, the funds were seen as seed capital, as characterized in the previous chapter. For further financial supply, the cell was on its own authority. In this respect, the New York assassin of 1993, Mohammed Salameh reclaimed the deposit sum of 400 USD for the rent truck to buy a flight ticket in order to leave the country; as a result, the US authorities apprehended the terrorists.[254] In total, the first attack of the World Trade Center which cost about 25,000 USD was financed by small-scale criminal activities such as credit card fraud.[255] The same applied to the bombers of Bali: The attack was estimated at 30,000 USD in preparation and execution costs, which partly originated from a robbery of a jewel store.[256]

Even the so far most expensive terrorist attack of 9/11 which is said to have costs about 500,000 USD, the operational cash was economically handled. The bulk of money was spent for flight lessons.[257] Besides that, the bombers who infiltrated the United States gradually since 1996 lived under fairly modest conditions: cheap accommodation, cheap food. Considering the vast sums they received from accounts in United Arab Emirates (UAE), luxury was largely estranged to the groups. Even the relatively expensive business seats (about 4,500 USD per each person) in the planes that were steered into the World Trade Center and the

---

p. 23.

[254] See Huband, Mark (2001): Bankrolling bin Laden. In: Financial Times, 28 November 2001
(http://specials.ft.com/attackonterrorism/FT3FJ5RJMUC.html). Visited on 23 March 2005.

[255] See Robinson, Jeffrey (2004): How Petty Crime Funds Terror. In: International Herald Tribune, 13 August 2004
(http://www.iht.com/articles/2004/08/13/edrobin_ed3_.php). Visited on 7 August 2005.

[256] See „Showdown im Stadion". In: Der Spiegel 1, p. 78.

[257] It is questionable why of all things, the bombers took their flight lessons in the United States where they could much easier attract attention, especially when one of the designated pilots became suspicious as he only wanted to learn the start of an aircraft. Why the group of Mohammed Atta did not acquired knowledge of starting a passenger plane not in Afghanistan where the group verifiable stayed before the attacks of 9/11? Eventually, the Taliban had their own airline.

Pentagon, were booked in order to be close to the cockpit.[258] Unused funds had to be transferred back. Transferred by ordinary bank branches, Mohammed Atta, head of the bombers remit twice 2,000 USD to UAE bank accounts before he made his way to Boston. Another 5,000 USD found its way back via money transmitter of the Western Union.[259]

Still, the attacks of September 11, 2001 remain unique not only in its effects to the international security policy because for all other terrorist actions linked to Islamic terrorism, the assassins financed themselves by criminal activities to cover expenses. In these cases, the offenders were involved either in drug or cigarette smuggling, in smuggling of goods in general, in document forgery, in credit card fraud, in robberies, in product piracy, or in illicit trade with pseudo ephedrine[260] and diamonds, which made the terrorist more susceptible for legal investigations.

Enlarging upon the illegal trade in gemstones, drugs and cigarettes in connection with the financing of Islamic terrorism, the next three subchapters will briefly deal with it. They are going to document the ad-hoc-alliances between the organized crime and terrorism.[261]

---

[258] See Gunaratna 2003, pp. 86.

[259] See Griffith, Victoria et al. (2001): How the Hijackers Went Unnoticed. In: Financial Times, 29 November 2001
(http://specials.ft.com/attackonterrorism/FT3LAJ6UMUC.html). Visited on 23 May 2005; See also "U.S. Wants International Bank Record Access", In: The Information Management Journal, July/August, p. 12.

[260] Pseudo ephedrines belong to the group of sympathotonics which also include met amphetamines, among others used as doping. See Cassella, Stefan D. (2004): Terrorism and the Financial Sector: Are the Right Prosecutorial Tools Being Used? In: Journal of Money Laundering Control Vol. 7, No. 3, p. 281. (Hereafter referred to as Cassella 2004.)

[261] See Münkler, Herfried (2003): Über den Krieg: Stationen der Kriegsgeschichte im Spiegel ihrer theoretischen Reflexion. Weilerswist, p. 234.

Illegal Trade in Gemstones

The illicit trade in diamonds and other gemstones of the Hezbollah in West Africa was already discussed in chapter three. Similar methods were practised by al-Qaeda whose center of illegal trade in gemstones was based in Tanzania and Sierra Leone. Countries such as these are traditionally exploited by civil war parties and/or terrorist-oriented organizations because of their immense resources of precious stones.[262] The illicit trade in diamonds or other jewels is used both to consolidate power and to the personal enrichment of the groups that are in possession of the mines. This replaces as far as possible the collapsed economy.[263] Thereby, countries like Sierra Leone fulfil the qualifications in order to be a destabilized state.[264] Terrorist-oriented groups benefit from this stage.

When in 1991 from Liberia, militias of the Revolutionary United Front (RUF) under the leadership of Foday Sankoh invaded the neighboring Sierra Leone; they first brought the diamond mining region in the surroundings of the city of Koidu under control. In the course of time, Liberia under RUF-friendly president Charles Taylor became a central transit point for arms that were exchanged for diamonds and then smuggled into the civil war regions. The reference person for those arms deals was the former Red Army officer, Viktor Bout who was catered from the remnants of deserted Soviet arsenals and kept virtually all African conflicts of the 1990s alive.[265]

Through the intermediaries Abdullah Ahmed Abdullah and Ahmed Khalfan Ghailani, the Afghan war veteran Ibrahim Bah

---

[262] See Falksohn, Rüdiger (2003): Die vierte Welt. In: Der Spiegel 29, p. 98.
[263] See Kaldor, Mary (2000): Neue und alte Kriege: Organisierte Gewalt im Zeitalter der Globalisierung. Frankfurt/Main, pp. 161.
[264] "When state failure becomes complete, the local currency falls out of favour, and some or several international currencies take its place. Money changers are everywhere, legal or not, and arbitrage becomes an everyday national pursuit." See Rotberg 2002, p. 89.
[265] See Winer 2002, p. 25.

who was trained in Lebanon in the camps of Hezbollah and later even trained Charles Taylor and Foday Sankoh in Lybia,[266] established contact to al-Qaeda in 1998. Both, Abdullah and Ghailani are to be considered as main figures responsible for the terror attacks in Kenya and Tanzania.[267] In this manner, al-Qaeda was presumably able to convert by drug deals obtained money into easy to carry valuables. The advantages of illicit trade in jewels are quite obvious: The transfer of assets by messengers is simplified, and the origin of the money will be disguised.[268] Additionally, this opened new opportunities to al-Qaeda to buy the gemstones far below of its market price as the official export from Sierra Leone was prohibited during the time of civil war until its end in 2002 resp. the trade in precious stones from the west African country was banned on the international markets. So al-Qaeda duplicated the concept of Hezbollah which was already involved in illicit transactions with diamonds in the 1980s.[269] In the meantime, the US embassy in Sierra Leone is certain that each year gemstones worth of 70 to 100 million USD leave the country illegally.[270]

The second centre of illegal gem trade in Africa was Tanzania. During the trial against the assassins of East Africa, one of the defendants, the former secretary of bin Laden Wadih el Hage stated quite clearly that he was jointly responsible for the setup of the gem trade in Tanzania.[271] For that reason, in the former stronghold of al-Qaeda, in Mombasa the companies Tanzanite King and Black Giant were established in order to buy the

---

[266] See Farah, Douglas (2005): A Protected Friend of Terrorism. In: Washington Post, 25 April 2005, p. A19.

[267] See Dohnanyi 2002, pp. 199.

[268] See Farah, Douglas (2001): Al Qaeda Cash Tied to Diamond Trade. In: Washington Post,
2 November 2001, p. A1.

[269] See "Hezbollah and the West African Diamond Trade". In: Middle East Intelligence Bulletin Vol. 6, June/July 2004, p. 6.

[270] See "Hezbollah Profiting from African Diamonds". In: Associated Press, 29 June 2004.

[271] See „Neuer Zeuge im Terrorprozess". In: Frankfurter Allgemeine Zeitung, 6 March 2001, p. 9.

gemstones from the mine workers and later sent to Dubai.[272] Already in 1997, el Hage's house in Nairobi was searched by a joint action of the FBI and Kenyan officials. In doing so, the investigators found a diary which provided information about the role of illicit trade with tanzanite and other gemstones in the financing of al-Qaeda.[273] Accordingly, about 90 percent of the tanzanite production left the country illegally for possible terrorist destinations.[274]

Drug Trafficking

While the final report of the National Commission on Terrorist Attacks Upon the United States and some other experts doubted the fact that al-Qaeda is potentially financed by revenues of drug trade,[275] there are increasing reports in favour of the opposite.[276] As a reason for a risen focus on drug smuggling, experts call the closure of charities which account for a significant part of the annual budget of al-Qaeda until 2001.[277] Besides it is hard to believe, that in Afghanistan the rest of the Taliban and al-Qaeda miss the proportional profits of the sale or smuggling of drug heading to West Europe and North America.[278] Though, recent figures prove that since 2001 in Afghanistan the poppy growing acreage were reduced to 21 percent, the production of opium, however, remains constant and is already as high as in they year

---

[272] See Pearl, Daniel (2002): Underground Trade. Much-smuggled Gem Called Tanzanite Helps Bin Laden Supporters. In: Cooper, Helene (ed.): At Home in the World: Collected Writings of Daniel Pearl from the Wall Street Journal. New York, p. 85.

[273] See United States of America vs. Usama bin Laden, et al. United States District Court, Southern District of New York, 21 February 2001, p. 1082.

[274] See Simpson, Glenn (2002): Diary Offers More on Tanzanite, Al Qaeda Link. In: Wall Street Journal, 24 January 2002, p. B1.

[275] See National Commission on Terrorist Attacks upon the United States (2004): The 9/11 Commission Report. New York, p. 171; Gunaratna 2003, p. 82.

[276] See Takeyh /Gvosdev 2002, p. 99.

[277] See Comras 2005, p. 7.

[278] About drug dealing in Afghanistan see Dorronsoro, Gilles (1999): Afghanistan: von Solidaritätsnetzwerken zu regionalen Räumen. In: Jean, Francois/Jean-Christophe Rufin (ed.): Ökonomie der Kriege. Hamburg, pp. 121-154.

2003.[279] It can be assumed that the remains of al-Qaeda, which jointly control with the still-present Taliban about 35 percent of the country,[280] have entered into purpose-optimized alliances with the local organized crime scene, as observed in South America in the past.[281]

The present terrorist groups are favoured by the fact that the stationed coalition forces of operation "Enduring Freedom" have so far no mandate to combat drug trafficking and poppy cultivation actively.[282] The German Criminal Police Office therefore supposes that Afghanistan still remains a blooming landscape for terrorism in the future and it alerts of a "threat of major dimension" since much of the drug revenues goes to the terrorists.[283]

Drug trafficking has become the main financial support of international terrorism.[284] Currently almost all Islamist groups defray their costs by cultivation and/or distribution of narcotics and in this manner, they co-operate with organized crime.[285] Indeed, many advantages can be gained from the smuggling of drugs (and other goods): First, the financing is secured with the sale of drugs, on the other, already existing routes can be used for transportation.

In this respect, the Moroccan group which were behind the attacks of Madrid on March 11, 2004, were actively involved in

---

[279] See interview with Hamid Karzai (2005). In: Der Spiegel 38, p. 113.

[280] See Baraki, Matin (2004): Afghanistan nach den Taliban. In: Aus Politik und Zeitgeschichte B48, p. 27.

[281] See Willems, Peter (2004): Opium Production Soars. In: The Middle East October, p. 49.

[282] See Schneider, Mark L. (2003): Colombia in Kabul. In: Washington Times, 4 December 2003 (http://www.washtimes.com/op-ed/20031203-091025-5374r.htm). Visited on 11 May 2005.

[283] See Dahlkamp, Jürgen (2003): Mohn, Steine, Scherben. In: Der Spiegel 46, p. 44.

[284] See Wandinger, Thomas M. (2001): Das Terrornetzwerk El Kaida unter Usama bin Laden. In: Politische Meinung No. 385, p. 59.

[285] See Zoroya, Gregg/Donna Leinwand (2004): Rise of Drug Trade Threat to Afghanistan's Security. In: USA Today, 27 October 2004, p. A1.

smuggling of hashish from North Africa to Western Europe. Along this path the dynamite entered Spain with which the trains were blown up in Madrid. The investigations following the attacks revealed the already performed solidarity between the organized crime and the international terrorism. Both parties were working hand in hand – one was satisfied with the accumulated profits, important for the other party was that the money was directed through clandestine channels in the right direction and hence the recipient could execute the assignment. In some cases, this symbiosis goes far beyond a simple contract, in which both parties benefit from working together: In the wake of investigations of the attacks in Casablanca in May 2003, the imam of Toledo was targeted by the authorities. He was said to have financed the bombings and to have worked collegially with his brother in Morocco who was the local drug lord of the Rif region until his arrest in 2000.[286]

Cigarette Smuggling

The most famous case of cigarette smuggling associated with the financing of terrorist groups was discovered in the United States. On July 21, 2000, under the code name "Operation Smoke Screen" the FBI stormed a house in Charlotte, North Carolina, where officials among others documents in Arabic, weapons and a vast number of cigarettes which were apparently smuggled to America. The investigators proved further contacts to Lebanon and to the Shiite Hezbollah against the smuggling ring. For years, the group supported the Hezbollah with illegally acquired profits either in terms of equipment such as night vision devices and navigations systems or simple cash.[287] The money was said to be reached the Middle East via indirect routes over Paraguay by charities and money transmitters.[288]

---

[286] See Blanche, Ed (2004): Multibillion Dollar Illicit Drugs Sales Fuel Terror Offensive. In: The Middle East November, p. 47.
[287] See Raphaeli, Nimrod (2003): Financing of Terrorism: Sources, Methods, and Channels. In: Terrorism and Political Violence Vol. 15, No. 4, p. 76.
[288] See Gunaratna 2003, p. 220.

In similar cases on January 10, 2002, authorities found in the cities of Detroit, Cleveland, Chicago, Phoenix and Las Vegas about 36 tons of pseudoephedrine, and 4.5 million USD in cash.[289] In both cases the authorities concluded that not precisely defined revenues from the smuggling operations were sent to radical-Islamic groups with anti-Western background. It is assumed that Hezbollah and Hamas by this means would earn much larger amounts as in the case of al-Qaeda.[290]

Meanwhile, the German customs confirmed that the revenue from illegal businesses with cigarettes has far exceeded that of the drug smuggling.[291] Already in 1992, the then Yugoslav president Milosevic had financed his war by smuggling cigarettes. Furthermore, the ETA was defamed to have ties to the smuggler mafia in Europe.[292] It is worth to add that even the private sector has a vital interest in the smuggling of cigarettes, because without the barrier of taxes larger amounts can be sold.[293]

The two briefly portrayed cases in the USA show that criminal activities make terrorists and their affiliates and sponsors visible for the investigating authorities. In cases of illegally acquired funds, it is questionable to speak specifically of terrorist funds, as they are actually criminally acquired funds in a legal sense. Therefrom the notoriously difficult to prove evidence that the funds are going to be used for terrorist purposes, does not need to be made. In the United States, the authorities accused terrorist not because of their terrorist background or their links with

---

[289] See "U.S. Drug Ring Tied to Aid for Hezbollah". In: New York Times, 3 September 2002, p. A16.

[290] See Raghavan, R. K. (2004): Targeting Terrorist Finances. In: Frontline Vol. 21, 23 October 2004 (http:www.frontlineonnet.com/fl2122/stories/20041105006213200.htm). Visited on 2 September 2005.

[291] See Neumann, Conny/Andreas Ulrich: Rauchen für den Krieg. In: Der Spiegel 8, p. 82.

[292] See ibid.

[293] See Balzli, Beat (2003): Gewinne ohne Grenzen. In: Der Spiegel 4, pp. 56-58.

terrorists, but rather for criminal offenses. For instance, the president of the US Benevolence International Foundation, an Islamic relief organization which probably functioned as al-Qaeda financier, is serving an eleven-year prison sentence after he was found guilty of money laundering.[294]

---

[294] See Basile 2004, p. 173.

6 MEANS OF TRANSFER TERRORIST FUNDS

As Jonathan Winer stresses, the financing of terrorism is regarded as a minor problem in the larger context of globalization.[295] With the globalization structures have been established within the international finance system, which essentially simplified the effort of terrorists. Into the continuously more complex becoming monetary system, funds with illegal sources were infiltrated that should be designed for terrorist objectives. While about twenty years ago financial transactions across borders cumbersome and often expensive, the locally-based money has become a global player and banks has grown to international finance conglomerates whose regulation is almost impossible.[296]

Technical innovations in the information and communication sector have played a part in contributing that financial transactions became a matter of seconds, and so, with the help of computer-driven data transfer systems the money moves to the

---

[295] See Winer 2002, p. 6.
[296] See ibid. pp. 11.

other end of the world.[297] The volume of international financial transactions increased steadily since the global trade grew faster than the global production. The in December 1999 by the German Bundestag established Inquiry Commission "Globalization of the World Economy – Challenges and Answers" concluded in its final report in 2002 that the deregulated financial markets would not only contribute to an increasing in prosperity, but also could be abused to finance the organized crime and terrorist attacks.[298] Thereby, there are policing difficulties to control the global financial markets. An increasingly perceived problem became short-term investments in which enormous sums are invested, and shortly to be withdrawn later. Since speculative financial instruments are preferred by the financial sector, it is apparent that the trade in foreign exchange and financial derivates has risen: "Of the daily on the forex market traded 1.2 trillion USD serve at most five percent the financing of commercial transactions and direct investments. The majority concerns speculation and arbitrage transactions between internationally operating financial institutions."[299]

Nowadays, investors decide upon aleatory and therefore highly risky investments.[300] This is particularly true for hedge funds, a special kind of commodity futures (e.g. raw materials purchasing) which is coupled with another on the same date scheduled business to hedge against price fluctuations (e.g. product sales).[301] With the "Law of the Investment System and the Taxation of

---

[297] See Ford, Peter (2001): Tough Trail of Terror's Money. In: Christian Science Monitor, 19 October 2001, p. 1.

[298] See Final Report of the Inquiry Commission: Globalisierung der Weltwirtschaft – Herausforderungen und Antworten. In: Deutscher Bundestag, 14th Legislative Period, Printed Matter 14/9200, p. 100.

[299] See ibid. pp. 17.

[300] Due to these facts, Johannes Varwick assumes a trend towards a "casino-capitalism". See Varwick, Johannes (1998): Globalisierung. In: Woyke, Wichard (ed.): Handwörterbuch Internationale Politik. Opladen, p. 115.

[301] More on the topic "hedge funds" see: Hetzer, Wolfgang (2003): Money Laundering and Financial Markets. In: European Journal of Crime, Criminal Law and Criminal Justice Vol. 11/3, pp. 275.

Investment Funds" (in brief: Investment Modernization Act),[302] passed on December 14, 2003, hedge funds were allowed to be established in Germany for the first time. Worldwide, nearly 6,000 hedge funds manage about 500 to 600 billion USD a year. More than half of them operate via off-shore centers because there they don't have to deposit annual financial statements and therefore, they are not object of checks and limits of national governments.[303]

For this reason, it is not entirely consistent why hedge funds were admitted in Germany by the on December 15, 2003, passed law; yet those investments attracted the FBI investigators' attention in September 2001 since they promise the greatest anonymity for investors. The client usually remains hidden as investments are made via intermediaries. Common banks, in contrast, cannot guarantee a protection of anonymity.[304] Hedge funds must be viewed as extremely high risky bets on future price trends in which option trading in oil and gold is particularly popular.[305] So, in 2001, the suspicion amplified in Europe that several persons of the legal finance sector were said to have made a fortune on the attacks of September 11, 2001. Ernst Welteke, former president of the German Federal Bank, speculated to that effect on September 23, 2001, that the option trading on the stock markets has "developed insubordinately". The same applied to the trading in securities of the by the attacks affected insurance and aeronautics industries.[306] In fact, in the week before the attacks of 9/11 a surprisingly high volume of

---

[302] See Bundesgesetzblatt I. p.2676: Investment companies are not credit institutions or financial services institutions defined by the Banking Act, since they perform no banking and financial services as defined in Section 1a, Point 2 of the Banking Act. Therefore, an equality of investment companies with the term of institution in Section 1, Point 4 of the Money Laundering Act was performed.

[303] See Roth Jürgen (2004): Ermitteln verboten: Warum die Polizei den Kampf gegen die Kriminalität aufgegeben hat. Frankfurt/Main, p. 236.

[304] See „FBI sucht Terrorgelder bei Hedgefonds". In: Frankfurter Allgemeine Zeitung, 22 November 2001, p. 17.

[305] See Balzli, Beat (2004): Gift fürs Geschäft. In: Der Spiegel 34, pp. 74.

[306] See „Unbotmäßiger Handel vor und nach dem 11. September". In: Frankfurter Allgemeine Zeitung, 24 September 2001, p. 1.

trading activities in these sectors has been observed: three times of the usual amount of British Airways shares changed hands on Thursday, to name just one example. According to Loretta Napoleoni, in the three days before September 11, 2001, the volume of put options exceeded to 285times of normal trading levels.[307] More than a suspicion, however, did not result: Options and futures transactions are regular instruments on the financial markets.[308]

Already more than a week after the attacks on September 19, 2001, the accredited Israeli Institute for Counter-Terrorism published a report whereupon prior to attacks on the World Trade Center and the Pentagon insider trading must have been proceeding – without establishing a direct connection to the bombers (or their material principal).[309] Affected were businesses with so-called put options. Using these instruments, the traditional principle of stock buying conversed: If trader A can be sure a stock will lose value in future, he contacts market operator B and does not need to possess any stocks at that time (short selling). With operator B, he agrees on the parameters of the stock sale on a certain day, i.e. the value of the stock is fixed, regardless to its issue price on the agreed date. If the value drops, trader A is allowed to buy the stocks on the market before the due date in order to sell them later to operator B to the fixed price, which does not correspond to the actual value. Atypical behavior in trading with put options before the attacks, appeared

---

[307] See Napoleoni 2004, pp. 260.

[308] Similar businesses are one reason for the current high price for crude oil as bets are made on certain trends of prices through futures: The trade is carried out virtually for the most part, and even the capital expenditure for purchasing a certain amount of oil is very low. At the world's most important market place for raw materials, the New York Mercantile Exchange (Nymex), in this way the oil price boosted steadily without any visible link to the real offer. See Balzli, Beat (2004): Von der reinen Gier gesteuert. In: Der Spiegel 35, p. 78.

[309] See Radlauer, Don (2004): Black Tuesday: The World's Largest Insider Trading System? (http://www.ict.org.il/articles/articledet.cfm?articleid=386). Visited on 12 December 2004. See also Ringshaw, Grant (2001): Profits of Doom. In: The Sunday Telegraph, 23 September 2001 (http://www.news.telegraph.co.uk/money/main.jhtml?xml=/money/2001/09/23/ccter23.xml). Visited on 5 April 2005; Hafner 2002, pp. 104.

particularly in those industries that were directly (airlines, aircraft manufactures) or indirectly (insurance, re-insurance) affected by 9/11. Thus, the proportion of put options significantly prevailed compared with that of call options trading with stocks of American Airlines, United Airlines or, for example, of Morgan Stanley Dean Witter & Co which had rent 22 floors of the World Trade Center. To date, the identity of these dealers who obviously had insider knowledge has not been proven and there is little prospect that they will be prosecuted in the not so distant future: The transaction were made for a larger proportion from off-shore centers which set the anonymity of their customers to top priority.[310]

Official Money Transfer Systems

With the decline of state-sponsored terrorism, terrorist networks revert to illegal revenues. Similar to organized crime, global acting terrorist networks are interested in hiding the illegal origins of the money.[311] In this case, terrorist organizations adopt methods of money laundering.[312]

Resulting from the analysis of known cases of money laundering it became clear that certain concepts run the same procedure: While the phase model of Paolo Bernasconi included only the

---

[310] See König, Johann-Günther (2004): Die Finanzen des Osama bin Laden: Mit professionellem Geldmanagement und Schattenbanken finanziert sich der internationale Terrorismus, in: Frankfurter Rundschau online, 27 March 2004 (http://www.frankfurterrundschau.de/uebersicht/alle_dossiers/politik_ausland/t error_gegen_den_westen/das_netzwerk_al_qaeda/?cnt=411494&#top). Visited on 3 April 2005.

[311] See Thachuk 2002, p. 1.

[312] Probably the most popular and most common explanation was given by the investigation report of the President's Commission on Organized Crime in 1984 after which money laundering was seen as a process to conceal the existence of illegal profits and their sources, and is then looking for to make it appear declared as legal. Consequently, the illegal funds were categorized according to the existence, the illegal origin and the illegal use of income: "Money laundering is the process by which one conceals the existence, illegal source, or illegal application of income, and then disguise that income to make it appear legitimate." Quoted in Werner, Thomas Achim (1996): Wachstumsbranche Geldwäsche: Die Ökonomisierung der organisierten Kriminalität. Berlin, p. 14. (Hereafter referred to as Werner 1996.)

level one and two, the direct infiltration of illegal profits in the financial system and the subsequent back-and-forth-transfer of the money,[313] the three-phase-model of money laundering was more innovative and named concrete practices of money launderers. This model was developed by the US customs office in cooperation with the on the G7 congress in Paris founded Financial Action Task Force on Money Laundering (FATF) in 1989, and has been used as standard since it offers strategies to combat money laundering and funding terrorism. In addition, the model works well for picturing the whole complex of money laundering including its cross-linking with the legal international economic. This model is divided into the phases: placement stage (placement of money), layering stage (veiling) and integration stage (return of legitimate money).

The first stage is about channeling resp. placing of the through criminal activities incurred small bills into the financial system, and therefore into electronic payment transactions. Doing so, different paths are taken. On one side, by amounting below certain thresholds (e.g. € 15,000 in Germany, 10,000 USD in the USA), deposits of dirty money to bank accounts can be made since identification and reporting requirements of banks to competent authorities had been ceased by these amounts.[314] On the other, businesses such as restaurants, used car dealers, casinos or currency exchange offices are used for money laundering, which typically take large amounts in cash.[315] This will allow it to reduce the payment

---

[313] See Bernasconi, Paolo (1989): Finanzunterwelt: Gegen Wirtschaftskriminalität und organisiertes Verbrechen. Zurich, Wiesbaden, pp. 29.

[314] Despite national and international control measures against money laundering, banks remain primary target of money launderers because only deposit money allows a quick reaction on the global financial markets. See Suendorf, Ulrike (2001): Geldwäsche: Eine kriminologische Untersuchung. Neuwied, p. 162.

[315] In addition, the FATF counts front companies (companies with no business purpose), pretext individuals (use of family members for financial transactions), the misuse of credit cards, cash smuggling and the use of telegraphic transfer services to the techniques and methods which terror organizations have been used for the purpose of financial transfers in the past.

risks.[316] For law-enforcement, this phase is crucial as it still has close links with the illegally acquired money. At a later date, the paper trail is barely comprehensible.

In phase two, the disguise of origins of the laundering money begins (layering stage). Here, the money is moved back and forth as often as possible. Popular destination of theses transfers are banking centers where maximum discretion is promised to customers. Especially in terms of anonymity, so-called off-shore centers (financial havens) pursue a very distinct policy. Regardless of the policy statement of the presidents of central banks of the Group of Seven countries in Basel in 1988, which obliged a principal cooperation of banks of the signatory countries with national and international law-enforcement authorities (such as the current FATF and Europol) without touching the banking confidentiality, off-shore centers permit complete anonymity to their customers.[317] Main characteristics of in off-shore centers operating banks in are:

- none or minimal taxes,
- none or minimal accounting obligation,
- none or minimal banking supervision,
- a strict discretion policy,
- the protection of private property,
- liberal currency transfer and
- the refusal of international legal assistance.[318]

According to Jürgen Storbeck, director of Europol, the total amount of funded capital in countries such as Cyprus, the Netherlands Antilles and Cayman Islands is estimated at about

---

See FATF/GAFI (2003): Bericht über Geldwäschetypologien, 14 February 2003, p. 10.

[316] See Pieth, Mark (1992): Bekämpfung der Geldwäsche: Modellfall Schweiz? Basel, Frankfurt/Main, pp. 13.

[317] See Weintraub, Sidney (2002): Disrupting the Financing of Terrorism. In: The Washington Quarterly 25, p. 55.

[318] See Werner 1996, p. 34.

25 trillion USD.[319] While these tax havens have aroused suspicion only with respect to organized crime in the period before September 11, 2001; after this prominent date, off-shore centers appeared in another light since terrorist groups benefited from the guaranteed financial anonymity.[320]

After complete fogging of the funds' origin and the ongoing transactions, the money laundering enters the final stage, i.e. the money breaks away from the financial circuit. From this stage the criminal origin of funds becomes vaguely perceptible. The laundering process, however, is just complete when the money is attached with a legal background (integration stage). So far, the third stage plays a tangential role of the terrorists' considerations because their goal is not the increase of capital, but the use of funds in different places around the world.

Alternate Remittance Systems – Unofficial Money Transfers Systems – *hawala*

By definition of the Financial Action Task Force, unofficial money and value transfer systems operate beyond the conventional banking system.[321] The money remittance transactions are implemented without recourse to banks.[322]

---

[319] See Storbeck, Jürgen: Geldwäsche und organisierte Kriminalität. In: Transnationale organisierte Kriminalität und Geldwäsche – Parasit der Weltwirtschaft, p. 21 (http://www.spdfraktion.de/cnt/rs/rs_datei/0,,409,00.pdf). Visited on 21 February 2004.

[320] See Stein, Peter (2001): Internationale Finanzverflechtungen im Kontext der Globalisierungsdebatte. In: Politische Studien 380, p. 18.

[321] See FATF/GAFI: Bericht über Geldwäschetypologien 2002-2003, pp. 15.

[322] Alternate payment systems in Germany are financial services, defined by paragraph 1, point 1, No. 6 of the Banking Act, which are offered by non-licensed service providers. In Germany, the Banking Act is the legal basis for remittance transactions. Paragraph 1, point 1a states:"Financial service institutions are enterprises which provide financial services to other professionally or to an extent which requires a commercially organized business, and those are no credit institutions." Unlike countries without very strong banking systems, alternate remittance systems are money transfer businesses, and thus subject to approval. Commercially operating financial transactions may only be permitted upon written consent of the Federal

Depending on specific ethnic groups, underground banking is translated either with *hawala* (Arabic: trust), *Phoe Kuan / feiqian* (Chinese: flying money) or with *hundi* (Urdu or the Indian *hoondie*: exchange, debenture). This kind of money transfer predominates especially in crisis regions which lack a stable banking system (e.g. Afghanistan, Pakistan) or in regions, where the banking system remains exempt from regulatory actions (including Singapore, the Philippines, and mainly Malaysia). The method known as *hawala* is very common in the financing of international terrorism. However, millions of immigrant worker in the Middle East, Europe and North America utilize this tradition without being linked to any terrorist organization.

The *hawala* transfer invented to safely transport money by caravans which were highly vulnerable to attacks by bandits along the Silk Road (from China to Syria). It came from a time when the Arabic and Persian region did not yet have any geo-strategic importance due to its rich oil reserves, but this region only represented a transit way for the trade of the Western powers with East Asia.[323] This method proved to be extremely effective if someone wanted the money to be reached to the recipient safely and completely, but also still hiding the sender. Even the CIA practiced the alternate payment system to fund the commanders of the respective mujahedin groups (including the one day before 9/11 murdered Tajik Ahmed Shah Masood and the subsequent Afghan Prime Minister Gulbuddin Hekmatyar) during the clandestine struggle against the Soviet military occupation in Afghanistan in the 1980s. This was due to the fact that the US intelligence was not allowed to contact Afghanistan directly. Primary point of contact for covert assistance in Afghanistan was the Pakistani Inter-Service Intelligence Directorate (ISI).[324]

Financial Supervisory Authority (BaFin). The authority for supervision of financial transfers is also resident in the BaFin.

[323] See Ulfkotte 2001, p. 153.

[324] See Coll 2004, p. 152.

The modern concept of a *hawala* transfer is very simple. It requires usually only a laptop, a cell phone, a specific location (such as a restaurant or an currency exchange office) and the confidence of the contracting parties among themselves. For instance, a London-based Pakistani who wants to be sent some of his earned money to his family in Karachi turns to a local well-known *hawala* dealer and hands over the money (in this case, English pound). In return, the immigrant worker receives a password or code and pay to the dealer a commission of one or two percent of the transfer. Then, the two make phone calls to Pakistan: The dealer, or *hawaladar*, informs his colleagues about the amount and the identification number of the transferred money. By telling his relatives, the guest worker does exactly the same. One of these relatives can now move on to the broker in Karachi and after announcing the password, he/she gets the money from London – now withdrawn in rupees. Altogether, the transaction took no longer than the call of the two persons in London.[325]

Of the in total six billion USD, transferred to Pakistan each year, only 1.2 billion enter the country via the traditional banking system. The World Bank estimates that 50 percent of private money transfers in 2000 were made using the *hawala* system.[326] The benefits that accrue to the financing of international terrorism are obvious: For international transfers the *hawaladar* budgets very low costs. As commission the broker keeps only one or two percent of the transfer. In contrast, conventional banks require up to 15 percent. But most importantly, the *hawala* transactions are not documented.[327]

In the most affected countries such as India or Pakistan, *hawala* transfers are illegal.[328] Local regulations prohibit speculation in

---

[325] See Balzli, Beat (2002): Die Hydra Hawala. In: Der Spiegel 37, p. 87.

[326] See Abuza, Zachary (2003): Funding Terrorism in Southeast Asia. In: Contemporary Southeast Asia Vol. 25, No. 2, p. 184.

[327] See El-Samalouti 2004, p. 208.

[328] See Frantz, Douglas (2001): Ancient Secret System Moves Money Globally. In: New York Times, 3 October 2001, p. B5.

domestic currency. Transactions may only be offered at the official exchange rate and the provider must hold a license for it. The situation is different in the United Arab Emirates: Such financial transactions beyond the official exchange rate are generally allowed in Dubai. This enables many foreign guest workers (mostly from India and Pakistan) to send their savings at low cost to their families back home.[329] For this reason, a large numbers of Pakistani and Indian businessmen have settled to the Emirates or have offices there, the more so as Dubai is center of the local gold trade. Gold, diamonds and other precious stones (such as the blue tanzanite) are perfect currencies for terrorists: Easy to smuggle and easy to put into cash. It is thus no surprise that according to official US import statistics, the main gold mining areas are in Dubai and most of the diamonds were not found in South Africa but in the United Kingdom.[330] So it may be assumed, that these raw materials have been smuggled into these countries.

According to a working paper of the US Financial Intelligence Unit (Financial Crime Enforcement Network, FinCEN) in cooperation with Interpol, such transfers (whether *hawala* or *hundi*) are very difficult to control, because advertisements for these services are published in the newspapers of the migrant communities with flimsy terms like "Sweet Rupee Deals".[331] In addition, the transactions are documented only to a minimum or made in localities which hardly to seem to be a bank. As Udo Ulfkotte stressed, the scheme is based on a codex, which is older

---

[329] According tot he former US Deputy Secretary of the Treasury, Kenneth Dam, it is not a goal of international efforts to ban the hawala trade entirely (probably mindful of the fact that the hawala trade could be hardly banned or at least, this would have little effect). Eventually, quite a few people, including many foreign workers, are relying on alternate remittance systems beyond the traditional banks. See „Neue Fahndung nach Terrorgeldern". In: Frankfurter Allgemeine Zeitung, 12 June 2002, p. 15.

[330] See Riebsamen, Hans (2004): Wenn die Diamanten aus England kommen, in: Frankfurter Allgemeine Sonntagszeitung, 7 November 2004, p.45.

[331] See Jost, Patrick M./Harjit Singh Sandhu (2002): The Hawala Alternative Remittance System and its Role in Money Laundering, 2 October 2002, (Prepared by the Financial Crime Enforcement Network), p.11.

than all banks around the world: the word of a man.[332] The structures of the hawala transfers are embedded in family, friendly or business relationship between the parties themselves. The trust refers not only to those who occupies the service of the money transfer and gives the money to the dealer (*hawaladar* or *hundiwala*) in order that he calls his business partner in oversea. The respective money trader must come to an arrangement among themselves.[333] In the medium to long term, there is a need for settlement if transfers from a richer to a poorer region were made. In this case, money traders fall back on money transmitter or on the export of goods that are needed in the destination country.[334] Cash couriers use quite often the same routes of drug or arms smugglers.[335]

After US emissaries apparently achieved little in the years 1999 and 2000, the UAE widely match the demands of Washington now, in order that the sheikdom adapts the regulations of the domestic banking system to the international standards of the FATF and its 40 recommendations.[336] The Central Bank of the UAE agreed at the International Conference on Hawala in May 2002 (jointly with the International Monetary Fund) on both, to ensure compliance of the 40 FATF recommendations – including the in 2001 formulated eight special recommendations on terrorist financing – and to a uniform registration and

---

[332] See Ulfkotte 2001, p. 155.

[333] The atmosphere of mutual trust cannot be pronounced often enough – especially in the Middle East. In this respect for instance, the Pakistani terrorist group Jaish-e-Mohammed has never had an own banking account, but it deposited money in the form of bestowals into private accounts so that its assets could not be frozen. See Pearl, Marianne: Ein mutiges Herz: Leben und Tode des Journalisten Daniel Pearl, Frankfurt/Main, p. 97.

[334] See „Hawala – Geldüberweisungen ohne Spuren". In: Neue Zürcher Zeitung, 31 May 2002 (www.nzz.ch/2002/05/31/wi/page-article86PF2.html). Visited on 15 May 2004.

[335] See Greenberg, Maurice R. (2002): Terrorist Financing: Report of an Independent Task Force Sponsored by the Council on Foreign Relations. New York, p. 11.

[336] See Farah, Douglas (2002): Al Qaeda's Road Paved with Gold: Secret Shipments Traced through a Lax System in United Arab Emirates. In: Washington Post, 17 February 2002, p. A1.

monitoring of *hawala* dealers.[337] These steps were urgently needed because despite the fact that the UAE in contrast to other countries in the Middle East had at least basic anti-money-laundering standards, Dubai was one of the largest financial centers of Islamic terrorists: From there, 100,000 USD were sent to the 9/11 bombers[338] and in 1998, the attacks in East Africa were financed via the Dubai Islamic Bank.[339]

To prohibit alternate remittance systems is not only an administrative impossibility, and would push *hawaladars* to attend their business underground and would thereby evade government supervision. A possible ban would also have serious implications for various economies. Estimates for 2003 have shown that a total of around 93 billion USD were sent through alternate remittance systems.[340] Many less-developed countries heavily rely on remittances by workers abroad. In Jordan, for example, those payments amount to one quarter of gross

---

[337] See United States Department of State: Patterns of Global Terrorism 2003, p. 69.

[338] About a fifth of the sum, which was necessary for organizing and implementing the attacks of 9/11, resulted of a ransom action. A report by the Los Angeles Times, which referred to the largest Indian weekly magazine India Today, pointed to a link of Dubai and Mohammed Atta to the United States. According to that, 100,000 USD came from India and were part of a ransom of 830,000 USD. In July 2001, the Indian shoe manufacturer Partha Roy Burman was kidnapped by a local Indian network of Asif Raza Khan and was kept imprisoned close to the border of Bangladesh. This network also included a man named Aftab Ansari (also known as Aftab Malik) who had close connections with the Bangladeshi Harkat-ul-Jihad-i-Islami and the Pakistani Harkat-ul-Mujahideen. Both were signatories of the fatwa of bin Laden in February 1998 at the announcement of the terrorist international. In prison he got to know the British-born Omar Saeed Sheikh. After serving out his sentence, Ansari moved to Dubai, but kept in touch with Saeed Sheikh until summer of 2001. In cooperation with Raza Khan, Ansari wanted to expand the network specialized in kidnapping from Dubai. Between August and September 2001, a bank transfer of around 100,000 USD was sent from the United Arab Emirates to the United States: Ansari had been given some of the ransom to Omar Saeed Sheikh who transferred it to an account of the Sun Bank. Account holder was Mohammed Atta. See Watson, Paul (2002): Deadly Shooting in Calcutta May Be Linked to Al Qaeda. In: Los Angeles Times, 23 January 2002, p. A11.

[339] See Winer 2002, p. 25.

[340] See "Monetary Lifeline". In: Economist, 31 July 2004, p. 66.

domestic product.[341] Alternate remittance systems are often the only way for foreign workers to support their families back home financially with small amounts if they are illegal immigrants who are not able to open bank accounts.

---

[341] See ibid.

7 OPTIONS FOR THE FIGHT AGAINST THE FINANCING OF TERRORISM

For a long time, terrorist organizations profited from the disunity of their enemies. To date, the international community could not agree on a common formula that clearly defines the term of "terrorism". This means a central problem in the fight against the international terrorism. What is punishable – only the financial support of the military wing of organizations such as Hamas or Hezbollah, or even of the political arm?[342] Beyond the debate whether terrorist or guerilla fighter, the terrorist organizations were able to expand their networks. They established their own profit-oriented companies, cooperated with charity organizations, utilized so-called failed states as refuge, and they fell back on criminal activities.

Both, the sources of funding and the options for transfer emphasize that the Islamic terrorism, besides its revenues from criminal activities, benefit to a large extent from the support of non-state actors. This trend has been already observed occasionally in the 1970s (PLO) and has been ripen in the late

---

[342] See "The Iceberg Beneath the Charity". In: Economist Vol. 366, 15 March 2003, p. 66.

1980s (Hezbollah). With the end of the Cold War and the systemic East-West antagonism, known "rogue states" such as Syria, Iraq or Iran reduced or even closed down their financial contribution to relevant terrorist organizations.[343] To compensate this situation, terrorist organizations focused on the expansion and the exploitation of other funding sources. Currently these include non-state actors such as Diaspora communities, wealthy individuals, charitable organizations, and spiritual authorities.

On the other hand, terrorist organizations contacted organized crime in order to diverse their sources. As Jens van Scherpenberg stressed, this is not an organic cooperation since the organized crime is interested in conserving the status quo for the accumulation of its own profits.[344] The terrorists, however, seek to destabilize or destroy state structures for certain political objectives. But recently, earmarked alliances of both parties have been observed. This may be due to the fact that terrorist organizations will increasingly difficult rely on revenues from apparent legal sources like charities since it came into focus of international investigations after September 11, 2001. In addition, criminal activities guarantee much higher profits: Presently, the International Monetary Fund estimates the amount of laundered money to two to five percent of the global gross national product. This represents an average of 800 billion to two trillion USD.[345] The by the US Treasury banned assets amounting to 140 million USD appear vanishingly small facing these sums.[346] That implies that even freezing of all terrorist-linked funds would only

---

[343] As known sources of funding al-Qaeda illustrated, a clear separation of state and non-state support is problematic, since part of the money came from people who were linked to Saudi governmental authorities. See Schneckener 2002, p. 35.

[344] See Scherpenberg, Jens van: Der Kampf gegen die Verflechtung von organisierter Kriminalität und Terrorismus (www.dgap.org/attachment/36292e5f08f727196eb4ca1f3d4df243/e8e4e53628 49225b7311ad51388b/scherpenberg.pdf). Visited on 8 September 2005.

[345] See Weintraub 2002, p. 54.

[346] See Zarate, Juan Carlos (2004): Bankrupting Terrorists. In: Economic Perspective Vol. 9, No. 3, September 2004, p. 6.

slightly restrict the global terrorism in its effect, if terrorists expand their relations with the organized crime. And in contrast to Cicero's dictum "nervos belli, pecuniam infinitam" (Philipicae orationes V, section 2.5), modest sums meet the terrorists' requirements to succeed their plans.

Conclusions for the Fight against the Financing of Terrorism

Although good progress on several fronts was made, al-Qaeda and other terrorist organizations continue to have access to financial resources. This fact represents an acute threat to the international community. So far, the issue of financing terrorism has not yet been solved.[347]

Various international forums are involved in a wide range of multilateral activities. A report by the New York Council on Foreign Relations advocated the founding of a new international organization which should exclusively address the issue of terrorist funding.[348] The urgency of global cooperation in this sector has been increasingly recognized by each of those countries that have joined the fight against terrorism:

- In September 2001, only four countries ratified the International Convention for the Suppression of the Financing of Terrorism; in April 2004, the number of countries has risen to 117.[349]
- The Counter-Terrorism Committee (CTC) of the United Nations (UN), which was established by

[347] See Greenberg, Maurice (Chair): Update on the Global Campaign Against Terrorist Financing: Second Report of an Independent Task Force on Terrorist Financing Sponsored by the Council on Foreign Relations, New York, 15 June 2004. (Hereafter referred to as Greenberg 2004.)

[348] See Greenberg, Maurice (Chair) (2002): Terrorist Financing: Report of an Independent Task Force Sponsored by the Council on Foreign Relations, New York, p. 27.

[349] To see the current status of the convention:

http://untreaty.un.org/english/bible/englishinternetbible/partI/chapterXVIII/treaty 11.asp.

Security Council Resolution 1373 (2001) requires all member states the introduction of financing terrorist groups into the national legislation as a criminal offense and the freezing of terrorist assets as a consequence. The biggest impact of the efforts of the UN generated the formation of domestic institutions such as the Financial Intelligence Units (FIU). In cooperation with the World Bank, the CTC of the UN provides assistance in introducing the financing of terrorism in the respective national legislation as a criminal offense, in establishing the FIUs, and in supporting bodies for the regulation of banking systems.[350]

- The FATF plays a major role in combating the financing of terrorism. In response to the attacks of 9/11, it added nine other recommendations dealing with the financing of terrorism to its agenda in addition to the existing 40 recommendations of the global fight against the money laundering.[351] Beside this, guidelines have been created to help individual countries to develop practices to freeze terrorist assets.[352] The meaning of alternate remittance systems is also in the focus of the task force as well as the importance of non-profit organizations associated with the financing of terrorist groups.

- The al-Qaeda/Taliban Sanction Committee, formed on the basis of UN Security Council Resolution 1267 (1999), has extent its list of terrorist individuals and organizations, and it is now able to provide member states with detailed information.

---

[350] See Greenberg 2004, p. 15.

[351] See FATF: Nine Special Recommendations on Terrorist Financing (http://www.fatf-gafi.org/document/9/0,2340,en_32250379_32236920_34032073_1_1_1_1,00.html). Visited on 12 January 2004.

[352] See FATF: Freezing of Terrorist Assets: International Best Practises, 3 October 2003; FATF: Guidance for International Institutions in Detecting Terrorist Financing, 24 April 2002.

- In cooperation with the FATF, the International Monetary Fund (IMF) and the World Bank examined within a pilot project 41 countries about their compliance with international standards to combat money laundering and terrorist funding. This was based on the "40+8 Recommendations" of the FATF. Especially for Germany, the IMF report concluded that a number of measures were taken, but the still pending ratification of the UN Convention for the Suppression of the Financing of Terrorism of 1999 and the lack of regulation to fight the support of funds for respective terrorists were reminded.[353]
- Cooperating in the field of financing terrorism has become a permanent part of the agendas of regional organizations such as the European Union (EU), the Asia-Pacific Economic Cooperation (APEC), the Association of Southeast Asian Nations (ASEAN), the Gulf Cooperation Council (GCC) and the African Union (AU).

The existence of apparent legal and illegal sources has straight consequences for the fight against terrorist funding. Sources like charitable organizations or private donors represented reliable absolute term to the terrorist organizations. The work of charities was not affected. Rather influential persons in the atmosphere of state governments participate in financing terrorism. Due to lax or missing regulation, Islamic organizations and banks in the Middle East were able to financially support the implementation of the objectives of terrorist organizations such as al-Qaeda, Hamas or Hezbollah.

---

[353] See Internationaler Währungsfonds: Deutschland: Bericht über die Befolgung von Standards und Codes. FATF-Empfehlungen zur Bekämpfung der Geldwäsche und der Terrorismusfinanzierung, Report of IMF No. 04/213, July 2004, p. 3.

No single country can tackle the fight against the terrorist financing on its own. Especially the United States and the EU are called for a closer collaboration with the countries of origin of terrorists such as Saudi Arabia, in particular to regulate the work of Islamic charities and the using of alternate remittance systems. The International Conference on Hawala in Abu Dhabi on May 15, 2002 and its follow-up meeting on April 5, 2004, has proven the first attempts for regulations and dictated the state registration of hawala dealers.

Countries like Saudi Arabia have already agreed on cooperation with the US intelligence and have taken a number of measures to curb terrorist financing at the same time. This included the criminalization of money laundering and terrorist financing in the national legislation, the establishment of an FIU, an improved log archiving of financial transfers, and licensing measures for alternate remittance systems.[354]

In spite of these measures that have been taken in the wake of the attacks of May 2003 in Riyadh, the fight against terrorist financing remains deficient in Saudi Arabia. In the recent years, not even a single sued trial versus alleged financiers of terrorist groups became prominent - at least none that was accessible to the public.[355] Individuals such as Yasin al-Qadi (Muwafaq), Wa'el Hamza Jalaidan (Muslim World League, Rabita Trust)[356] and Akil

---

[354] See Royal Embassy of the Kingdom of Saudi Arabia: Initiatives and Actions Taken by the Kingdom of Saudi Arabia in the War on Terrorism, September 2003
(http://www.saudiembassy.net/2003News/News/TerDetail.asp?cIndex=142). Visited on 15 July 2005.

[355] „We have found no evidence that Saudi Arabia has taken public punitive actions against any individual for financing terror. As a result, Saudi Arabia has yet to demand personal accountability in its efforts to combat terrorist financing and, more broadly and fundamentally, to delegitimize these activities." See Greenberg 2004, pp. 17.

[356] According tot he Saudi embassy in Washington, in the summer of 2002, steps were taken to freeze the assets of Wa'el Hamza Jalaidan. Whether this was actually done and what assets this may be, remains unclear. The report of January 2005 does not mention any further actions against the person of Jalaidan. See Royal Embassy of the Kingdom of Saudi Arabia: Initiatives and

al-Akil (al-Haramain Foundation) who were clearly identified as supports of terrorism by the US Treasury, continue living unhindered by Saudi judiciary.

Two years after the actual onset of the Saudi anti-terror campaign, there is a gap between demand and reality. The Saudi royalty knows exactly that it is an exquisite objective for terrorist attacks. According to a confidential survey conducted by the government, about 49 percent of the Saudi population still supports the ideas of bin Laden.[357] Also forgotten is the former export of the Saudi persuasion and its put emphasis on radical elements which assisted Islamic groups in their creation and supported them financially sometimes by the government. Only focus on its own past and more rigorous and transparent actions against alleged financiers of terrorist groups should be the prerequisite for a successful fight against terrorism which can no longer be kept by paying certain sums to the respective Islamists at a save distance from the Arab peninsula.

A much bigger issue of the future might be the fight against the illegal sources of terrorism since it is assumed that the cooperation between terrorists and criminals expands to that extent as the dying up of the apparent legal sources of terrorism proceeds. The terrorists will continue to privatize their financial resources and there is obvious suspicion that smaller cells will fund through criminal activities soon. This "entrepreneur-terrorism" might have only little outward resemblance to the network of al-Qaeda which distributed the funds to each affiliated group. Even today, in the eyes of smaller terrorist groups, al-Qaeda possesses the characteristics of being little more of an "ideological reference".[358]

Actions Taken by the Kingdom of Saudi Arabia in the War on Terrorism, January 2005, p. 14 (http://www.saudiembassy.net/ReportLink/WOT-January-2005.pdf). Visited on 15 July 2005.
[357] See Zakaria, Fareed (2004): The Saudi Trap. In: Newsweek Vol. 143, 28 June 2004, p. 31.
[358] See Cziesche, Dominik et al. (2005): "Schwert und Blut". In: Der Spiegel 28, p. 30.

As a result of the knowledge about the financial structures of terrorist groups after September 11, 2001, facing the seemingly legitimate generation of funds by donations from individuals, governments (or government officials) and non-profit organizations, and the use of alternate remittance systems, some experts thought that international law and practices to contain money laundering are not applicable to the financing of terrorism. They spoke a "reverse money laundering" because the money was not acquired illegally to a large part.[359] For this reason, on June 30, 2004, the European Commission adopted and submitted a proposal for a "Directive of the European Parliament and the Council on the Prevention of the Use of the Financial System for the Purpose of Money Laundering and the Financing of Terrorism" (Third Money Laundering Directive).[360] By doing so, the current definition of money laundering should be adapted to the recent trends in order that a definition "in future includes not only the manipulation of money derived from crime but also the merging of legal funds and lawful properties for terrorist purposes".[361]

Legally spoken, a distinction between terrorist and criminal money makes no sense if it originates from criminal activities since the term "terrorist money" tries to cover an undone offense.[362] Indeed, this circumstance exposes to be a bigger issue,

---

[359] In a report by the French National Assembly, the representative Andrè Rouviere described the funding of terrorism as "reverse money laundering". See Cohen, Laurie P.et al. (2001): Bush's Financial War on Terrorism: Includes Strikes at Islamic Charities. In: Wall Street Journal, 25 September 2001, p. A1.

[360] In the first Money Laundering Directive of 1991, member states were obliged to prohibit money laundering of proceeds from drug trafficking, furthermore, to identify customers, to keep all relating documents and to notify all suspicious transactions to the respective authorities. In the second Money Laundering Directive, funding terrorism was not explicitly addressed though. Yet the countries agreed on the fact that all crimes linked to the funding of terrorism must be seen as "serious crime". See Hetzer, Wolfgang (2004): Europäische Strategien gegen Geldwäsche und Terror. In: Aus Politik und Zeitgeschichte B44, p. 28.

[361] See Kommissionsvorschlag (KOM) (2004) 448 endgültig, p. 10.

[362] See Robinson, Jeffrey (2004): How Petty Crime Funds Terror. In: International Herald Tribune, 13 August 2004

because a reference to terrorist financing can usually only be made after the appropriate actions have already been executed. In this respect, in Germany and other countries, the legislatures amended various laws according to current issues and qualified the financing of terrorist organization as a criminal offense.[363] So far for the investigating authorities was it therefore important that the acquired money derived from crime, with the amendment of the Money Laundering Act on August 8, 2002,[364] the use of funds will be tracked.

In 2004, the German FIU noticed in its annual report that only two percent of all received suspicions of money laundering were based on financing terrorism. And only 16 criminal complaints from there were filed because of the suspicion of financing terrorist associations.[365] As the report also stressed, members or supporters of criminal organizations were rarely sentenced based on financing terrorism, but in many cases for criminal offenses.[366] That means, the fight against terrorism does not have do be necessarily declared as such. Incriminated funds of terrorists can also be seized with tools to combat money laundering without providing the proof of financing terrorist organizations. Usually it is sufficient that the money derives from an illegal origin in order to verify extended lapse (Section 73d

---

(http://www.iht.com/articles/2004/08/13/edrobin_ed3_.php). Visited on 7 August 2005.

[363] Overall, in Germany money laundering and financing terrorism are treated separately under criminal law. A criminal offence explicitly called of financing terrorism is not available in Germany, but the judiciary relies on Section 129 of the Criminal Code "Forming a Terrorist Group", i.e., the German Money Laundering Act which was amended on August 8, 2002, does not include an extension of Section 261 of the Criminal Code that defines the previous convictions of money laundering. This means that in Germany although the support of domestic and foreign terrorist organizations is prosecuted, whereas the financial support of individuals has met no response. In this case, the regulations for conspiracy to commit a crime and the Section 27 of the Criminal Code are intended for aiding.

[364] See Bundesgesetzblatt I of 14 August 2002, pp. 3105.

[365] See Bundeskriminalamt: Jahresbericht 2003. Financial Intelligence Unit (FIU) Deutschland. Wiesbaden, p. 32.

[366] See ibid.

German Criminal Code) or confiscation (Section 74a German Criminal Code).[367]

A similar trend is also observed in the United States where in the context of the on October 24, 2001, by the Congress adopted law "Uniting and Strengthing America by Providing Appropriate Tools Required to Intercept and Obstruct Terrorism" (USA PATRIOT Act), a series of laws were amended. These included Title 18, United States Code (USC), Section 981 (a)(1)(G), 18, USC, § 2339A and 18, USC, § 2339B which deals with the support of terrorist groups that are listed by the US Department of the State. Besides this, two laws already exist that were adopted within the fight against money laundering to prevent both criminal and terrorist actions:

1. 18, USC, § 1956 (a)(2)(A): Concerning offenses if the money is transferred abroad to support a crime of any nature financially.
2. 18, USC, § 1960: This paragraph is focused on persons or organizations which do business national and international as so-called money transmitter and need to be licensed.

To combat the financing of terrorist organizations, the already existing legislative measures remain practicable. In some cases, the apply of the new regulations seems to be not strictly necessary since a violation of law can be proved more easily with already existing legal situation. The case of Yehuda Abraham in the United States can shortly illustrate this.

In August 2003, the point of prosecution against Hemant Lakhani, an arrested arms dealer, was reached. He was alleged of smuggling surface-to-air missiles into the USA to New Jersey. These missiles were thought to be used against civil airplanes.

---

[367] This especially applies to financial investigations aimed at the identification and seizure of assets in criminal proceedings. In doing so, options for disorgements or for a possible return to the victims (sequestration) are to be determined. However, if the lapse of assets is expressed by the respective court at the main trial as a consequence, the property of the assets confers on the state.

The weapons came from remnants of the Soviet army. The various payments for the rockets were made through an intermediary in New York. Yehuda Abraham, diamond dealer and according to his own statements experienced in utilizing alternate remittance systems, received a commission of 1,500 USD for the initial transfer of 60,000 USD to a Swiss bank account and should later send additional 500,000 USD for 50 more missiles. According to this, Abraham was guilty under paragraphs 2339A and 1956 (a)(2)(A) because he knowingly forwarded money for terrorist purposes to a second individual resp. he supported a crime abroad. The easiest way was, however, to design the indictment after 18, USC, Section 1960: Abraham held no license for his transfers for a second individual and was sentenced to a five year imprisonment. That means, he and his accomplices had not to be proven activities of terrorist offenses.[368]

It became clear that the laws that were adopted in the wake of the Patriot Act 2001 were formally correct and particularly important, but its application is usually difficult. 18, USC § 981 (a)(1)(G) states that all funds on accounts of listed terrorist organizations are banned immediately without any evidence. So in the unlikely situation, Osama bin Laden would try to open a bank account in New York, the deposited fund would be frozen on the very same day. But what about the front companies whose address in the letterhead is not named with "Terrorism Ltd."? What happens to those funds that are invested beyond US American and European competences? For this reason, it should be in the interest of all in the global fight against terrorism participating nations to support the core countries of Islamic terrorism with logistical support.

---

[368] See Cassella 2004, p. 284.

8 BIBLIOGRAPHY

Books

- Adams, James (1990): Wer finanziert den Terror? Die geheimen Geldgeber terroristischer Organisationen. Bergisch Gladbach, *Luebbe Verlagsgruppe.*
- Allan, Pierre/ Dieter Kläy (1999): Zwischen Bürokratie und Ideologie: Entscheidungsprozesse in Moskaus Afghanistankonflikt. Bern, Stuttgart, Vienna, *Paul Haupt Verlag.*
- Aust, Stefan/ Cordt Schnibben (ed.) (2002): 11. September. Geschichte eines Terrorangriffs. Stuttgart, Munich, *DVA.*
- Baer, Robert (2003): Die Saudi-Connection: Wie Amerika seine Seele verkaufte. München, *Bertelsmann.*
- Barber, Benjamin R. (1996): Coca Cola und Heiliger Krieg: Wie Kapitalismus und Fundamentalismus Demokratie und Freiheit abschaffen. Bern, Munich, Vienna, *Scherz Verlag.*

- Bergen, Peter L. (2003): Heiliger Krieg Inc.: Osama bin Ladens Terrornetz. Berlin, *BVT Berliner Taschenbuch Verlag.*
- Bernasconi, Paolo (1989): Finanzunterwelt: Gegen Wirtschaftskriminalität und organisiertes Verbrechen. Zurich, Wiesbaden, *Orell Füssli Verlag.*
- Bodansky, Yossef (1999): Bin Laden: The Man Who Declared War on America. Roseville, *Prima Lifestyles.*
- Brisard, Jean-Charles/ Guillaume Dasquiè (2003): Die verbotene Wahrheit: Die Verstrickungen der USA mit Osama bin Laden. Hamburg, *Rowohlt Taschenbuch.*
- Chomsky, Noam (2002): The Attack: Hintergründe und Folgen. Hamburg, *Europa Verlag.*
- Clarke, Richard A. (2004): Against All Enemies: Der Insiderbericht über Amerikas Krieg gegen den Terror. Hamburg, *Hoffmann und Campe.*
- Clausewitz, Carl von (2002): Vom Kriege. Hamburg, *rororo.*
- Coll, Steve (2004): Ghost Wars: The Secret History of the CIA, Afghanistan, and bin Laden, from the Soviet Invasion to September 10, 2001. New York, *Penguin (Non-Classics).*
- Cooper, Helene (ed.) (2002): At Home in the World: Collected Writings from the Wall Street Journal. New York, *Simon & Schuster.*
- Demandt, Alexander (ed.) (1996): Das Attentat in der Geschichte. Cologne, Weimar, Vienna, *Böhlau Verlag.*
- Emerson, Steven (2003): American Jihad: The Terrorists Living Among Us. New York, *Free Press.*
- Frank, Hans/Kai Hirschmann (ed.): Die weltweite Gefahr: Terrorismus als internationale Herausforderung. Berlin, *Berliner Wissenschafts-Verlag.*
- Gunaratna, Rohan (2003): Inside al-Qaeda: Global Network of Terror. New York, *Berkley Trade.*

- Hafner, Wolfgang (2002): Im Schatten der Derivate: Das schmutzige Geschäft der Finanzelite mit der Geldwäsche. Frankfurt/Main, *Eichborn Verlag*.
- Henry, Clement M./Rodney Wilson (ed.) (2004): The Politics of Islamic Finance. Edinburgh, *Edinburgh University Press*.
- Hirschmann, Kai (2003): Terrorismus. Hamburg, *Europäische Verlagsanstalt*.
- Hoffman, Bruce et al. (2001): Trends in Outside Support for Insurgent Movements. Santa Monica, *Rand Corporation*.
- Hoffman, Bruce (1999): Terrorismus – der unerklärte Krieg: Neue Gefahren politischer Gewalt. Frankfurt/Main, *Fischer Verlag*.
- International Monetary Fund (ed.) (2003): Suppressing the Financing of Terrorism. A Handbook for Legislative Drafting, Washington.
- Jäggi, Christian J./ David J. Krieger (1991): Fundamentalismus. Ein Phänomen der Gegenwart. Zurich, Wiesbaden, *Orell Füssli*.
- Jean, Francois/ Jean-Christophe Rufin (ed.) (1999): Ökonomie der Bürgerkriege. Hamburg, *Hamburger Edition*.
- Kaldor, Mary (2000): Alte und neue Kriege: Organisierte Gewalt im Zeitalter der Globalisierung. Frankfurt/Main, *Suhrkamp Verlag* .
- Kennedy, Paul (1994): Aufstieg und Fall der großen Mächte: Ökonomischer Wandel und militärischer Konflikt von 1500 bis 2000. Frankfurt/Main, *Fischer Taschenbuch Verlag*.
- Kepel, Gilles (2004): Das Schwarzbuch des Dschihad: Aufstieg und Niedergang des Islamismus. Munich, *Piper*.
- Khella, Kharam (1982): Der israelisch-arabische Konflikt: Über Krieg und Frieden im Nahen Osten. Hamburg, *Theorie und Praxis*.

- Krautkrämer, Elmar (2003): Krieg ohne Ende? Israel und die Palästinenser – Geschichte eines Konflikts. Darmstadt, *Primus Verlag.*
- Labeviere, Richard (2000): Dollars for Terror: The U.S. and Islam. New York, *Algora Publishing.*
- Laqueur, Walter (2001): Die globale Bedrohung: Neue Gefahren des Terrorismus. Munich, *Econ.*
- Laqueur, Walter (1997): Faschismus. Gestern – Heute – Morgen. Berlin, *Propyläen.*
- Laqueur, Walter (2004): Krieg dem Westen: Terrorismus im 21. Jahrhundert. Berlin, *Ullstein.*
- Lerch, Wolfgang Günter (1991): Allahs neue Krieger. Braunschweig, *Westermann.*
- Lewis, Bernard (1994): Der Atem Allahs: Die islamische Welt und der Westen – Kampf der Kulturen? Vienna, Munich, *Europa Verlag.*
- Lewis, Bernhard (2003): Die Wut der arabischen Welt: Warum der jahrhundertelange Konflikt zwischen dem Islam und dem Westen weiter eskaliert. Frankfurt/M., New York, *Campus Verlag.*
- Münkler, Herfried (2003): Über den Krieg: Stationen der Kriegsgeschichte im Spiegel ihrer theoretischen Reflexion. Göttingen, *Velbrück.*
- Napoleoni, Loretta (2004): Ökonomie des Terrors: Auf der Spur der Dollars hinter dem Terrorismus. Munich, *Kunstmann.*
- Pearl, Marianne (2004): Ein mutiges Herz: Leben und Tod des Journalisten Daniel Pearl. Frankfurt/Main, *Scherz Verlag.*
- Pieth, Mark (ed.) (2002): Financing Terrorism. Dordrecht, Boston, London, *Springer Netherlands.*
- Pieth, Mark (1992): Bekämpfung der Geldwäscherei: Modellfall Schweiz?, Basel, Frankfurt/Main, *Helbing & Lichtenhahn.*
- Rashid, Ahmed (2001): Taliban: Afghanistans Gotteskrieger und der Dschihad. Munich, *Droemer Knaur.*

- Robinson, Adam (2002): Bin Laden: Behind the Mask of the Terrorist. New York, *Arcade Publishing.*

- Rosly, Saiful Azhar (2005): Critical Issues on Islamic Banking and Financial Markets: Islamic Economics, Banking and Finance, Investments, Takaful and Financial Planning. Bloomington, *Authorhouse* .

- Roth, Jürgen (2004): Ermitteln verboten: Warum die Polizei den Kampf gegen die Kriminalität aufgegeben hat. Frankfurt/Main, *Eichborn.*

- Scheuer, Michael (2005): Imperial Hubris: Why the West Is Losing the War on Terror. Dulles, *Brassey's.*

- Scheuer, Michael (2003): Through Our Enemies' Eyes: Osama bin Laden, Radical Islam, and the Future of America. Washington, *Brassey's.*

- Schmid, Alex P. (1988): Political Terrorism: A New Guide to Actors, Authors, Concepts, Data Bases, Theories, and Literature. New Brunswick, *Elsevier Science Ltd.*

- Schmid, Alex (1983): Political Terrorism. Amsterdam, *Elsevier Science Ltd.*

- Sterling, Claire (1983): Das internationale Terrornetz: Der geheime Krieg gegen die westlichen Demokratien. Bergisch Gladbach, *Luebbe.*

- Suendorf, Ulrike (2001): Geldwäsche: Eine kriminologische Untersuchung. Neuwied, *Luchterhand.*

- Sunderbrink, Ute (1993): Die PLO in der Krise? Genese, Strukturmerkmale und Politikmuster der Palästinensischen Befreiungsorganisation und deren Herausforderung durch den politischen Islam in der Intifada. Münster, Hamburg, *LIT.*

- Taylor, Paul D. (ed.) (2004): Latin American Security Challenges. A Collaborative Inquiry from North and South, Newport, *Government Printing Office.*

- Ulfkotte, Udo (2003): Der Krieg in unseren Städten: Wie radikale Islamisten Deutschland unterwandern. Frankfurt/Main, *Eichborn.*

- Ulfkotte, Udo (2001): Propheten des Terrors: Das geheime Netzwerk der Islamisten. Munich, *Goldmann Verlag*.
- Voigt, Rüdiger (ed.) (2002): Krieg – Instrument der Politik? Bewaffnete Konflikte im Übergang vom 20. zum 21. Jahrhundert. Baden-Baden, *Nomos Verlagsgesellschaft*.
- Warde, Ibrahim (2000): Islamic Finance in the Global Economy. Edinburgh, *Columbia University Press*.
- Warg, Gunter (2002): Terrorismusbekämpfung in der Europäischen Union. Speyer, *DHV*.
- Werner, Thomas Achim (1996): Wachstumsbranche Geldwäsche: Die Ökonomisierung der organisierten Kriminalität. Berlin, *edition sigma*.
- Wippel, Steffen (1995): „Islam" und „Islamische Wirtschaft": Vertreter des religiösen und politischen Islam und der islamischen Wirtschafts- und Wohlfahrtseinrichtungen in Ägypten. Berlin, *Freie Universität Berlin*.

Articles

- Abdelkarim, Riad Z. (2004): After Year of Uncertainty: American Muslim Charitable Donations Rebound. In: Washington Report on Middle East Affair Vol. 23, January/February, pp.62-64.
- Abuza, Zachardy (2003): Funding Terrorism in Southeast Asia: The Financial Network of Al Qaeda Jemaah Islamiya. In: Contemporary Southeast Asia Vol. 25, No. 2, pp. 169-199.
- Alexiev, Alex (2004): Ölmilliarden für den Dschihad: Saudi-Arabien finanziert den globalen Islamismus. In: Internationale Politik 2, pp. 21-28.
- Andreas, Peter/Richard Price (2001): From War Fighting to Crime Fighting: Transforming the American

National Security State. In: International Studies Review Vol. 3, Fall 2001, pp. 31-52.

- "Angriffe auch auf Lager der Hizbullah?" In: Frankfurter Allgemeine Zeitung, 29 November 2001, p. 4.
- Aversa, Jeannine (2004): Bush Administration Accuses Saudi Charity of Financing Terrorism. In: Associated Press, 9 September 2004.
- Balzli, Beat (2002): Die Hydra Hawala. In: Der Spiegel 37, pp. 86-87.
- Balzli, Beat (2003): Gewinne ohne Grenzen. In: Der Spiegel 4, pp. 56-58.
- Balzli, Beat (2004): Gift fürs Geschäft. In: Der Spiegel 34, pp. 74-76.
- Balzli, Beat (2001): Guter Muslim. In: Der Spiegel 46,
- p. 110.
- Balzli, Beat (2004): Von der reinen Gier gesteuert. In: Der Spiegel 35, pp. 78-80.
- Baraki, Matin (2004): Afghanistan nach den Taliban. In: Aus Politik und Zeitgeschichte B48, pp. 24-30.
- Baraki, Matin (2002): Islamismus und Großmachtpolitik in Afghanistan. In: Aus Politik und Zeitgeschichte B8, pp. 32-37.
- Bartolome, Mariano Cesar (2002): La Triple Frontera: Principal Foco de Inseguridad en el Cono Sur Americano. In: Military Review, July-August, pp. 61-74.
- Basile, Mark (2004): Going to the Source: Why al Qaeda's Financial Network Is Likely to Withstand the Current War on Terrorist Financing. In: Studies in Conflict and Terrorism 27, pp. 169-185.
- Blanche, Ed (2004): Multibillion Dollar Illicit Drugs Sales Fuel Terror Offensive. In: The Middle East November, p. 47.
- Brück, Tilman/Dieter Schumacher (2004): Die wirtschaftlichen Folgen des internationalen Terrorismus. In: Aus Politik und Zeitgeschichte B3-4, pp. 41-46.

- Bush, Janet (2004): America's Foes Prepares for a Monetary Jihad. In: The Newstatesman, 4 October 2004, pp. 34-35.
- Cassella, Stefan D. (2004): Terrorism and the Financial Sector: Are the Right Prosecutorial Tools Being Used? In: Journal of Money Laundering Control Vol. 7, No. 3, pp. 281-285.
- Cohen, Laurie P. Et al. (2001): Bush's Financial War on Terrorism Includes Strikes on Islamic Charities. In: Wall Street Journal, 25 September 2001, p. A1.
- Cole, Cassandra R./ Kathleen A. McCulough (2002): Excluding Terror. In: CPCU Journal Vol. 55, No. 6, August, pp. 1-7.
- Comras, Victor (2005): Al Qaeda Finances and Funding to Affiliated Groups. In: Strategic Insights Vol. IV, Issue I, January, pp. 1-16.
- Cooley, John K. (2002): Hawala und Tansanit: Die flüchtigen Gelder der al-Qaida. In: Le Monde diplomatique Nr. 6905, 15 November 2002, p. 16.
- Cooper, Barry (2002): Unholy Terror: The Origin and Significance of Contemporary, Religion-based Terrorism. In: Studies in Defence and Foreign Policy No. 1, March, pp. 1-50.
- Curtis, Glenn E. Et al. (2003): Nations Hospitable to Organized Crime and Terrorism: A Report Prepared by the Federal Research Division, Library of Congress under the Interagency Agreement with the United States Government, Washington, October.
- Cziesche, Dominik et al. (2005): "Schwert und Blut". In: Der Spiegel 28, pp. 28-34.
- Cziesche, Dominik et al. (2002): Attas Armee. In: Der Spiegel 36, pp. 110-123.
- Dahlkamp, Jürgen (2003): Mohn, Steine, Scherben. In: Der Spiegel 46, pp. 42-44.
- „Das neue Monster in Afghanistan". In: Frankfurter Allgemeine Zeitung, 11 October 1996, p. 2.

- Duran, Khalid (1998): Geschäfte mit dem großen Satan. In: Frankfurter Allgemeine Zeitung, 26 May 1998, p. 10.
- Ehrenfeld, Rachel (2002): Where Does the Money Go? A Study of the Palestinian Authority. October 2002 (http://www.intelligence.org.il/eng/bu/financing/articl es/where/where.htm). Visited on 16 June 2005.
- Ehrke, Michael (2003): Erdöl und Strategie: Zur politischen Ökonomie eines angekündigten Krieges. In: Internationale Politik und Gesellschaft 1, pp. 9-23.
- Emerson, Steven (2003): Terrorism Financing: Origination, Organization, and Prevention. Saudi Arabia, Terrorist Financing and the War on Terror. Testimony Before the United States Senate Committee on Governmental Affairs, 31 July 2003.
- Enquete-Kommission: Abschlussbericht der Enquete-Kommission: Globalisierung der Weltwirtschaft – Herausforderungen und Antworten. In: Deutscher Bundestag, 14. Wahlperiode, Drucksache 14/9200.
- Falksohn, Rüdiger (2003): Die vierte Welt. In: Der Spiegel 29, pp. 94-100.
- Farah, Douglas (2005): A Protected Friend of Terrorism. In: Washington Post, 25 April 2005, p. A19.
- Farah, Douglas (2001): Al Qaeda Cash Tied to Diamond Trade. In: Washington Post, 2 November 2001, p. A1.
- Farah, Douglas (2002): Al Qaeda's Road Paved With Gold: Secret Shipments Traced Through a Lax System in United Arab Emirates. In: Washington Post, 17 February 2002, p. A1.
- „FBI such Terrorgelder bei Hedgefonds". In: Frankfurter Allgemeine Zeitung, 22 November 2001, p. 17.
- Fleischauer, Jan (2004): Puzzlearbeit im Schattenreich. In: Spiegel Special 2, pp. 36-39.
- Foxell Jr., Joseph W. (2003): The US War on Terrorism: Prospects for Success? In: American Foreign Policy Interests 25, pp. 177-198.

- Frantz, Douglas (2001): Ancient Secret System Moves Money Globally. In: New York Times, 3 October 2001, p. B5.
- Fröhlingsdorf, Michael (2004): Neuer Markt auf Türkisch. In: Der Spiegel 5, pp.36-38.
- "Funds Continue to Flow Despite Drive to Freeze Network's Assets". In: The Guardian, 5 September 2002 (http://www.guardian.co.uk/international/story/0,,7861 03,00.html#article_continue). Visited on 4.11.2004.
- "Geld für Terroristen aus den Golfstaaten". In: Frankfurter Allgemeine Zeitung, 16 August 1996, p. 5.
- Goldberg, Jeffrey (2002): In the Party of God. Hezbollah Sets Up Operations in South America and the United States. In: The New Yorker, 28 October 2002 (http://www.newyorker.com/fact/content/articles/021 028fa_fact2). Visited on 30 August 2005.
- Greenberg, Maurice (Chair) (2002): Terrorist Financing: Report of an Independent Task Force Sponsored by the Council on Foreign Relations. New York 2002.
- Greenberg, Maurice (Chair) (2004): Update on the Global Campaign Against Terrorist Financing: Second Report of an Independent Task Force on Terrorist Financing Sponsored by the Council on Foreign Relations. New York, 15 June 2004.
- Griffith, Victoria et al. (2001): How the Hijackers Went Unnoticed. In: Financial Times, 29 November 2001 (http://specials.ft.com/attackonterrorism/FT3LAJ6UM UC.html). Visited on 23 May 2005.
- Grossbongardt, Anette (2004): Die Millionen der Hamas. In: Spiegel Special 2, p. 102.
- „Hawala – Geldüberweisungen ohne Spuren". In: Neue Zürcher Zeitung, 31 May 2002 (www.nzz.ch/2002/05/31/wi/page-article86PF2.html). Visited on 15 May 2004.
- Hermann, Rainer (2001): Der Terrorist und sein Finanznetz. In: Frankfurter Allgemeine Zeitung, 29 September 2001, p. 15.

- Herrmann, Frank (1996): Osama bin Laden – der Bankier des Terrors. In: Berliner Zeitung, 28 October 1996, p. 6.
- Hetzer, Wolfgang (2004): Europäische Strategien gegen Geldwäsche und Terror. In: Aus Politik und Zeitgeschichte B44, pp. 28-32.
- Hetzer, Wolfgang (2003): Money Laundering and Financial Markets. In: European Journal of Crime, Criminal Law and Criminal Justice Vol. 11, 3, pp. 264-277.
- "Hezbollah and the West African Diamond Trade". In: Middle East Intelligence Bulletin Vol. 6, June/July, p. 6.
- "Hezbollah Profiting from African Diamonds". In: Associated Press, 29 June 2004.
- Holm, Carsten (2003): Hilfe für den großen Bruder. In: Der Spiegel 3, p. 34.
- Hosenball, Mark (2002): Terror's Cash Flow. In: Newsweek Vol. 139, 25 March 2002, pp. 28-30.
- Huband, Mark (2001): Bankrolling bin Laden. In: Financial Times, 28 November 2001 (http://specials.ft.com/attackonterrorism/FT3FJ5RJM UC.html). Visited on 23 March 2005.
- Hudson, Rex (2003): Terrorist and Organized Crime in the Tri-Border Area (TBA) of South America: A Report Prepared by the Federal Research Divison, Library of Congress under an Interagency Agreement with the United States Government, Washington 2003.
- Jost, Patrick M./ Harjit Singh Sandhu (2002): The Hawala Alternative Remittance System and its Role in Money Laundering, 2 October 2002, (Prepared by the Financial Crime Enforcement Network).
- Junger, Sebastian (2002): Terrorism's New Geography. In: Vanity Fair No. 508, December, pp. 194-206.
- Kaplan, David E./Monica Ekman (2003): The Saudi-Connection. In: U.S. News & World Report Vol. 135, 15 December 2003, pp. 18-27.

- Katzman, Kenneth (2002): Terrorism: Near Eastern Groups and State Sponsors, 13 February 2002 (CRS Report for Congress).
- Kelley, Jack (1999): Saudi Money Aiding bin Laden. In: USA Today, 29 October 1999, p. A1.
- Kestenholz, Daniel (2003): Saudisches Geld für indonesische Terroristen? In: Die Welt, 15 July 2003 (http://www.welt.de/data/2003/07/15/133989.html?prx=1). Visited on 3 December 2004.
- Khan, Nadim/Mohammed Paracha (2005): No Shortage of Interest. In: The Lawyer, 21 March 2005 (http://www.thelawyer.com/no-shortage-of-interest/114533.article). Visited on 23 June 2005.
- Khatab, Sayed (2002): Citizenship of Non-Muslims in the Islamic State of *Hakimiyya* Espoused by Sayyid Qutb. In: Islam and Christian-Muslim Relations Vol. 13, No. 2, pp. 163-187.
- Kiser, Steve (2005): Financing Terror: An Analysis and Simulation for Affecting Al-Qaeda's Financial Infrastructure. Santa Monica.
- Kocher, Viktor (2004): Saudisches Hilfswerk unter Anklage. In: Neue Zürcher Zeitung, 13 October 2004 (http://www.nzz.ch/dossiers/2003/terrorismus/2004.1 0.13-al-article9X2GH.html). Visited on 2 November 2004.
- König, Johann-Günther (2004): Die Finanzen des Osama bin Laden: Mit professionellem Geldmanagement und Schattenbanken finanziert sich der internationale Terrorismus. In: Frankfurter Rundschau online, 27 March 2004 (http://www.frankfurterrundschau.de/uebersicht/alle_d ossiers/politik_ausland/terror_gegen_den_westen/das_ netzwerk_al_qaeda/?cnt=411494&#top). Visited on 3 April 2005.
- Kraske, Marion (2003): In heiliger Mission. In: Der Spiegel 50, pp. 156-157.

- Kremp, Jürgen (2001): Gewalt gegen Gewalt. In: Der Spiegel 23, p. 154
- Kussbach, Erich (2003): Der Terrorismus und das internationale Strafrecht. In: Politische Studien Heft 387, 54. Jahrgang, Januar/Februar, pp. 61-85.
- Leavitt, Paul (2004): Rumsfeld: Iran, Iraq, Syria Back Terrorism. In: USA Today, 2 April 2004. p. A10.
- Leibfritz, Willi (2004): Auswirkungen des Terrorismus auf die Volkswirtschaften und die Wirtschaftspolitik. In: Aus Politik und Zeitgeschichte B3-4, pp. 47-54.
- Levitt, Matthew (2002): Charitable and Humanitarian Organizations in the Network of International Terrorist Financing: Testimony Before the United States Subcommittee on International Trade and Finance, 1 August 2002.
- Levitt, Matthew (2005): Hezbollah. Financing Terror through Criminal Enterprises. Hearing of the Committee on Homeland Security and Governmental Affairs United States. Washington, D.C. 2005.
- Levitt, Matthew (2002): The Political Economy of Middle East Terrorism. In: Middle East Review of International Affairs Vol. 6, No. 4, pp. 49-65.
- Lumpkin, John J. (2004): Insurgents Infiltrating Iraq Have Cash. In: Associated Press, 21 October 2004.
- Madani, Blanca (2002): Hezbollah's Global Finance Network: The Triple Frontier. In: Middle East Intelligence Bulletin Vol. 4, No. 1, January (http://www.meib.org/articles/0201_12.htm). Visited on 31 August 2005.
- Mascolo, Georg/Holger Stark (2003): Operation Heiliger Dienstag. In: Der Spiegel 44, pp. 120-135.
- Mascolo, Georg (2003): Die Saudi-Connection. In: Der Spiegel 14, pp. 70-72.
- Mascolo, Georg (2003): Verdächtig gezuckt. In: Der Spiegel 4, p. 37.

- Meehan, Howard Vincent (2004): Terrorism, Diasporas, and Permisseve Threat Environments: A Study of Hizballah's Fundraising Operations in Paraguay and Ecuador. Monterey 2004.
- Mendel, William W. (2002): Paraguay's Ciudad del Este and New Centers of Gravity. In: Military Review March-April, pp. 51-57.
- Mohan, Raja C. (2004): What If Pakistan Fails? India Isn't Worried...Yet. In: Washington Quarterly 28 (Winter 2004-05), pp. 117-128.
- "Monetary Lifeline". In: Economist, 31 July 2004, p. 66.
- Müller, Tilmann (1998): Die Terror GmbH. In: Der Stern 41, pp. 42-48.
- Münkler, Herfried (2003): Die Kriege des 21. Jahrhunderts. In: Gewerkschaftliche Monatshefte 4, pp. 193-204.
- „Neue Fahndung nach Terrorgeldern". In: Frankfurter Allgemeine Zeitung, 12 June 2002, p. 15.
- „Neuer Zeuge im Terrorprozess". In: Frankfurter Allgemeine Zeitung, 6 March 2001, p. 9.
- Nienhaus, Volker (2002): Islam und Staatlichkeit: Zur Vereinbarkeit von Religion, Demokratie und Marktwirtschaft. In: Internationale Politik 3, pp. 11-18.
- O'Donnell, Guillermo (1993): On the State: Democratization and Some Conceptual Problems (A Latin American View With Glances at Some Post-communist Countries). Working Paper #192 (University of Notre Dame, The Helen Kellogg Institute for International Studies, April 1993).
- O'Harrow, Robert et al. (2001): Bin Laden's Money Takes Hidden Paths To Agents of Terror. In: Washington Post, 21 September 2001, p. A13.
- Oltmanns, Jan: Definitions-Dilemma. Was ist Terrorismus? (http://tagesthemen.de/aktuell/meldungen/0,1185,OI D3355742_TYP1_NAVSPM3~3572754_REF1,00.html) . Visited on 10 September 2004.

- "Palestinians Aid". In: Middle East Reporter, 11 May 1982.
- Paz, Reuven (2000): Targeting Terrorist Financing in the Middle East: Paper Presented at the International Conference on Countering Terrorism through Enhanced International Cooperation Courmayeur, Mont Blanc, Italy, 24 September 2000 (http://www.ict.org.il/articles/articledet.cfm?articleid=137). Visited on 22 April 2005.
- Radlauer, Don: Black Tuesday. The World's Largest Insider Trading System? (http://www.ict.org.il/articles/articledet.cfm?articleid=386). Visited on 12 December 2004.
- Rao, Padma et al. (2001): "Wir dachten, nun ist alles aus". In: Der Spiegel 2, pp. 126-128.
- Raphaeli, Nimrod (2003): Financing of Terrorism: Sources, Methods, and Channels. In: Terrorism and Political Violence Vol. 15, No. 4, (Winter 2003), pp. 59-82.
- Riebsamen, Hans (2004): Wenn die Diamanten aus England kommen. In: Frankfurter Allgemeine Sonntagszeitung, 7 November 2004, p. 45.
- Ringshaw, Grant (2001): Profits of Doom. In: The Sunday Telegraph, 23 September 2001 (http://www.news.telegraph.co.uk/money/main.jhtml?xml=/money/2001/09/23/ccter23.xml). Visited on 5 April 2005.
- Robinson, Jeffrey (2004): How Petty Crime Funds Terror. In: International Herald Tribune, 13 August 2004 (http://www.iht.com/articles/2004/08/13/edrobin_ed3_.php). Visited on 7 August 2005.
- Rohter, Larry (2001): Terrorists Are Sought in Latin Smuggler's Haven. In: New York Times, 27 September 2001, p. A3.
- Rosenbach, Marcel/Michael Wulzinger (2003): Arabische Liga. In: Der Spiegel 6, pp. 70-73.

- Rößler, Hans-Christian (2003): Terroristen oder Wohltäter? In: Frankfurter Allgemeine Zeitung, 18 July 2003, p. 6.
- Rotberg, Robert I. (2002): The New Nature of Nation-State Failure. In: The Washington Quarterly 25, pp. 85-96.
- Rüb, Matthias (2002): Fremdkörper aus Saudi-Arabien. In: Frankfurter Allgemeine Zeitung, 25 March 2002, p. 6.
- Sachs, Susann (2001): An Investigation in Egypt Illustrates Al Qaeda's Web. In: New York Times, 21 November 2001, p. 1.
- Sanford, Jeff (2004): Muslim Profit. In: Canadian Business, 27 September 2004, p. 39.
- "Saudis Shut Down Charity". In: Al Jazeera Online, 5 October 2004 (http://english.aljazeera.net/NR/exeres/E358AE91-FAEC-407C-BDE9-31E80C0BA37B.htm). Visited on 2 November 2004.
- Schneckener, Ulrich (2002): Netzwerke des Terrors: Charakter und Strukturen des transnationalen Terrorismus. Studie der Stiftung Wissenschaft und Politik. Berlin 2002.
- Schneider, Friedrich (2001): Die Finanzströme islamischer Terror-Organisationen. Vorläufige Erkenntnisse aus volkswirtschaftlicher Sicht. Schriftliche Fassung eines eingeladenen Vortrages zum Symposium „Geldwäsche und verdeckte Terrorfinanzierung. Bedrohung der Staatengemeinschaft", veranstaltet vom Bundesnachrichtendienst, Pullach (BRD), 25.10.2001.
- Schneider, Mark L. (2003): Colombia in Kabul. In: Washington Times, 4 December 2003 (http://www.washtimes.com/op-ed/20031203-091025-5374r.htm). Visited on 11 May 2005.
- Seri, Guillermina S. (2003): On Borders and Zoning: The Vilification of the "Triple Frontier". Prepared for

Delivery at the 2003 Meeting of the Latin American Studies Association. Dallas 2003.

- Shahar, Yael (2001): Tracing bin Laden's Money: Easier Said than Done, Institute for CounterTerrorism, 21 September 2001 (http://www.ict.org.il/articles/articledet.cfm?articleid=3 87). Visited on 4 October 2004.
- „Showdown im Stadion". In: Der Spiegel 1, p. 78.
- Siddiqi, Moin A. (2002): Banking on Shari'ah Principles. In: The Middle East July/August, pp. 34-38.
- Simpson, Glenn (20029: Diary Offers More on Tanzanite, Al Qaeda Link: in: Wall Street Journal, 24 January 2002, p. B1.
- Stalinsky, Steven: Saudi Royal Family's Financial Support to the Palestinians 1998-2003: More than 15 Billion Riyals ($4 Billion U.S.) Given to 'Mujahideen Fighters' and 'Families of Martyrs'. In: Middle East Media Research Institute, Special Report No. 17 (http://memri.org/bin/opener.cgi?Page=archives&ID= SR1703). Visited on 30 July 2004.
- Stein, Lisa (2004): Charity or Front? In: U.S. News & World Report Vol. 136, 2 February 2004, p. 14.
- Stein, Peter (2001): Internationale Verflechtungen im Kontext der Globalisierungsdebatte. In: Politische Studien Heft 380, 52. Jahrgang, pp. 17-21.
- Steinitz, Mark S. (2003): Middle East Terrorist Activity in Latin America. In: Policy Papers on the Americas Vol. XIV, Study 7, July 2003.
- Takeyh, Ray/Nikolas Gvosdev (2002): Do Terrorist Networks Need a Home? In: The Washington Quarterly 25, pp. 97-108.
- Thachuk, Kimberley (2002): Terrorism's Financial Lifeline. Can It be Severed? In: Strategic Forum (Institute for National Strategic Studies National Defense University) No. 191, pp. 1-7.

- Thamm, Berndt Georg (2002): Kaderschmiede des islamistischen Terrorismus. In: Politische Studien Heft 381, 53. Jahrgang, pp. 56-74.
- "The Iceberg Beneath the Charity". In: Economist Vol. 366, 15 March 2003, pp. 67-69.
- The National Intelligence Council (2000): Global Trends 2015. A Dialogue About the Future With Nongoverment Experts. Washington.
- "U.S. Drug Ring Tied to Aid for Hezbollah". In: New York Times, 3 September 2002, p. A16.
- Ufen, Andreas (2004): Islam und Politik in Südostasien: Neuere Entwicklungen in Malaysia und Indonesien. In: Aus Politik und Zeitgeschichte B21-22, pp. 15-21.
- Ulfkotte, Udo (1996): Bildet Teheran in geheimen Lagern 5000 ausländische Terroristen aus? In: Frankfurter Allgemeine Zeitung, 8 August 1996, p. 6.
- Ulfkotte, Udo (2001): Treibt Riad ein doppeltes Spiel? In: Frankfurter Allgemeine Zeitung, 5 December 2001, p. 6.
- „Unbotmäßiger Handel vor und nach dem 11. September". In: Frankfurter Allgemeine Zeitung, 24 September 2001, p. 1.
- Valdmanis, Thor (2001): Family, Friends Tell of the Man Behind Bin Laden. In: USA Today, 12 October 2001, p. A13.
- „Vergebliche Warnungen". In: Der Spiegel 42, p. 107.
- Vidino, Lorenzo (2005): The Muslim Brotherhood's Conquest of Europe. In: Middle East Quarterly Winter, pp. 25-34.
- Vistica, Gregory L./Daniel Klaidman (1998): Tracking Terror. In: Newsweek Vol. 132, 19 October 1998, p. 46.
- Wandinger, Thomas M. (2001): Das Terrornetzwerk El Kaida unter Usama bin Laden. In: Politische Meinung No. 385, pp. 57-65.

- Warde, Ibrahim (2001): Eine unwahrscheinliche Erfolgsgeschichte. In: Le Monde Diplomatique, 14 September 2001, p.5.
- „Washington vermutet Terrorzellen in Südamerika". In: Frankfurter Allgemeine Zeitung, 19 October 2001, p. 8.
- Wassermann, Andreas (2003): Quelle CI1. In: Der Spiegel 27, p. 48.
- Watson, Paul (2002): Deadly Shooting in Calcutta May Be Linked to Al Qaeda. In: Los Angeles Times, 23 January 2002, p. A11.
- Weintraub, Sidney (2002): Disrupting the Financing of Terrorism. In: The Washington Quarterly 25, pp. 53-60.
- "Weitere Konten eingefroren". In: Frankfurter Allgemeine Zeitung, 9 November 2001, p. 7.
- Willems, Peter (2004): Opium Production Soars. In: The Middle East October, p. 49.
- Willman, John (2001): Trail of Terrorist Dollars that Spans the World. In: Financial Times, 29 November 2001 (http://specials.ft.com/attackonterrorism/FT3RNR3X MUC.html). Visited on 23 March 2005.
- Winchell, Sean P. (2003): Pakistan's ISI: The Invisible Government. In: International Journal of Intelligence and CounterIntelligence Vol. 16, No. 3, pp. 374-388.
- Zoroya, Gregg/Donna Leinwand (2004): Rise of Drug Trade Threat to Afghanistan's Security. In: USA Today, 27 October 2004, p. A1.
- Zuckerman, Mortimer B. (2002): Who Finances the Fanatics? In: US News & World Report Vol. 133, 30 December 2002, p. 92.

www.ingramcontent.com/pod-product-compliance
Lightning Source LLC
Chambersburg PA
CBHW072137280526
45788CB00002B/673